AFRICAN AMERICANS

COMING TO AMERICA

AFRICAN AMERICANS

DAVID BOYLE

Series editor: Barry Moreno

First edition for the United States, its territories
and dependencies, and Canada published in 2003
by Barron's Educational Series, Inc.

Copyright © 2002 by
THE IVY PRESS LIMITED

This book was created by
The Ivy Press Ltd., The Old Candlemakers, Lewes, East Sussex BN7 2NZ, UK

Creative Director Peter Bridgewater
Publisher Sophie Collins
Editorial Director Steve Luck
Design Manager Tony Seddon
Designer Andrew Milne
Senior Project Editor Caroline Earle
Editor Stephanie Schwartz-Driver
Picture Researcher Vanessa Fletcher

All inquiries should be addressed to:
Barron's Educational Series, Inc.
250 Wireless Blvd.
Hauppauge, NY 11788

www.barronseduc.com

International Standard Book No.: 0-7641-5628-4

Library of Congress Catalog No.: 2002112400

Printed and bound in China by Hong Kong Graphics and Printing Ltd

9 8 7 6 5 4 3 2 1

CONTENTS

INTRODUCTION

W. E. B. DU BOIS

"We are Americans, not only by our birth and by citizenship, but by our political ideals, our language, our religion. Farther than that, our Americanism does not go. At that point we are Negroes, members of a vast historic race that from the very dawn of creation has slept, but half awakening in the dark forests of its African fatherland. We are the first fruits of this new nation, the harbinger of a black tomorrow which is yet destined to soften the whiteness of the Teutonic today."

The history of African Americans is the history of America. Slavery, segregation, and their legacies have meant that the issue of race has dominated American history. The issue, never far from the surface, exploded in the 1860s with the Civil War, and again a century later in the 1960s with the Civil Rights movement. Both were the direct result of mistakes made in the 1660s when—led by Maryland and Virginia—the colonists forbade inter-marriage between the races and designated black people as slaves for life.

African Americans first set foot on North American soil before the *Mayflower* landed its cargo of Puritans escaping religious persecution in Europe. They were present at crucial moments in the birth of the new nation—Crispus Attucks, the first casualty of the American Revolution, was a free black living in Boston. And although many arrived in the new colonies involuntarily, the fact is that they arrived at the same time as the first white settlers did.

For many people, the physical process of emigration is an act of liberation, as they leave behind oppressive circumstances to travel to a new land of promise. But for the Africans who traveled to the New World in their thousands up until the ban on importing slaves was imposed in 1808, this was simply not the case. For them, emigration meant enslavement. They were wrenched involuntarily from their homes, or betrayed by traders who promised riches but delivered shackles. Then they made their voyages in chains, under conditions that no words can fully describe— untold thousands died during the Atlantic crossing. And following their arrival at their new homes, they were forced into an existence often harder to bear than the murderous journey had been.

LEFT: *Cruelty and severe physical punishment were often the norm for African slaves.*

LEFT: *For the thousands of Africans imported to the United States prior to 1808, the New World would be one of enslavement and misery.*

RIGHT *This statue commemorated the liberation of slaves, but African Americans still had a long way to go before they were truly "free."*

LEFT: *Educator, writer, and champion of rights for African Americans, Booker T. Washington (1856–1915).*

BELOW *In the face of intense opposition, African Americans fought for— and won— the right to vote.*

Names, religion, cultural identity were stolen from them, and their lives were redefined and subjugated.

Thus, the story of the African-American journey – of "coming to America"—is in two parts. The first story tells of the grief and horror of forced expatriation, and of discovering the "peculiar institution" that was the American slave system. That they managed to survive, to fight for freedom, to procreate, to create, is an achievement described by writer Ralph Ellison as "one of the great human experiences and one of the great triumphs of the human spirit in modern times, in fact, in the history of the world."

8

The second part of the journey is still taking place. It is the long, complex process of fighting for freedom and equality—the pillars on which America was founded—and redefining African-American identity on its own terms.

Along the way, the contribution made by African Americans over the centuries to the cultural and political landscape of the United States is incalculable. Despite often violent attempts to segregate and subjugate the African-American spirit, it has always proved to be unquenchable. It is African Americans to whom American culture owes much of its vibrancy and creative fire. The African contribution to American culture is so fundamental that it is often impossible to isolate or to define—but it is certainly something to celebrate.

LANGSTON HUGHES

"Refugee in America"

*"There are words like Freedom
Sweet and wonderful to say.
On my heart-strings
freedom sings
All day everyday.*

*There are words like Liberty
That almost make me cry.
If you had known
what I knew
You would know why."*

DANGER
EDUCATED
BLACKWOMAN

SLAVERY

OLAUDAH EQUIANO

"One day, when all our people were gone out to their works as usual, and only I and my dear sister were left to mind the house, two men and a woman got over our walls, and in a moment seized us both; and, without giving us time to cry out, or make resistance, they stopped our mouths, and ran off with us into the nearest wood."

That was how the eighteenth-century freed slave turned abolitionist Olaudah Equiano described the moment he was seized from the Ibo tribe in West Africa to be sold into slavery. "Here they tied our hands, and continued to carry us as far as they could, till night came on, when we reached a small house, where the robbers halted for refreshment, and spent the night. We were then unbound; but were unable to take any food; and, being quite overpowered by fatigue and grief, our only relief was some sleep, which allayed our misfortune for a short time."

Equiano's grim account was one that had already become familiar. It would become even more so, as millions more Africans discovered for themselves the horrors of the Middle Passage, as the journey from the coast of West Africa to the New World came to be known.

The story of African Americans in the New World is much older than the slave trade itself. Archeological evidence from Colombia shows the presence of Africans in Central and South America. This suggests that Africans made the journey to America long before Christopher Columbus, and that slaves were transported to South America even earlier than to the European colonies in the north. The first documented slaver

to and in North America was a nameless Dutch man-of-war, arriving in Jamestown, Virginia, in 1619, that robbed a Spanish slave ship of its cargo of Africans. This happened one year before the voyage of the *Mayflower*.

A new era begins

Two of the 20 Africans on board, who were given the Spanish names Antoney and Isabella, fell in love, married, and had a child who was baptized into the Church of England. Although they were not the first of their race on American soil, their arrival marked the beginning of the modern history of black America.

THE SLAVE TRADE

Of the millions of people sent in chains from Africa up until the mid-nineteenth century, around half arrived in the New World (the rest went to Europe). Most departed from a 3,000-mile stretch of the West African coast. These people were captured from their inland villages by fellow Africans. They were to be sold at auction to the European slave traders who moored off the coast, waiting until they had purchased a full load.

Once on board, conditions were extreme. In order to fit the maximum number of people onto the ship, Africans were packed into shelves in the hold, sometimes no more than 18 inches high, for the ten-week-long transatlantic voyage. They were allowed only a few minutes a day up on deck (weather permitting). There they were forced to "dance," to jump and move so that their legs would not atrophy, which would reduce their value. Many would die on the way from dysentery, suicide, or violence. The mortality rate was between 10 and 20 percent for each crossing. Their bodies were thrown overboard; sharks were said to follow the slave ships all the way across the Atlantic.

The ships would first dock either in the Caribbean or in Brazil, where a further set of auctions was held. George Washington is recorded as having purchased a male slave by mail order for $260 from one of these auctions. The Africans were haggled over as if they were merchandise. "You call this buck 20 years old? Why there's cut worms in

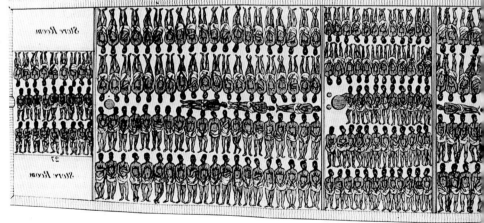

RIGHT: *Slave traders packed their ships tightly to increase their profits during the Middle Passage, the journey across the Atlantic. For the slaves, conditions were inhumane.*

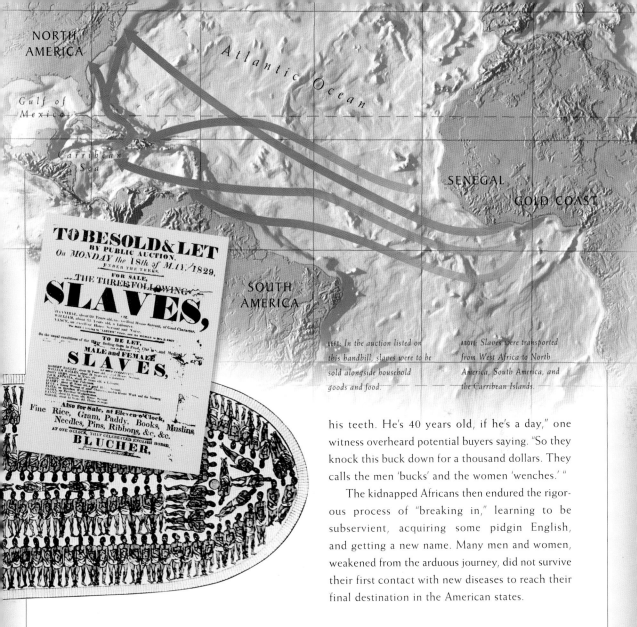

NORTH
AMERICA

Atlantic Ocean

Gulf of
Mexico

Carribean
Sea

SENEGAL

GOLD COAST

SOUTH
AMERICA

TO BE SOLD & LET
BY PUBLIC AUCTION.
On MONDAY the 18th of MAY, 1829,
UNDER THE TREES,
FOR SALE,
THE THREE FOLLOWING
SLAVES,

HANNIBAL, about 30 Years old, an excellent House Servant, of Good Character.
WILLIAM, about 35 Years old, a Labourer.
NANCY, an excellent House Servant and Nurse.

The men belonging to "LEECH'S" Point, are to remain a MAN & WIFE.

On the usual conditions of the Hirer finding them in Food, Clothes, and Medical

TO BE LET
MALE and FEMALE
SLAVES,

ROBERT BAGLEY, about 20 Years old, a good House Servant.
WILLIAM BAGLEY, about 18 Years old, a Labourer.
JOHN ARMS, about 18 Years old, a Labourer.
JACK ANTONA, about 40 Years old, a Labourer.
HARRY, about 27 Years old, a Labourer.
CHARLES, about 40 Years old, a House Servant.
FLORA, an Excellent Washerwoman, and in House Work and the Nursery.
FANNY, about 35 Years old, House Servant.
SARAH, about 11 Years old, House Servant.

Also for Sale, at Eleven o'Clock,
Fine Rice, Gram, Paddy, Books, Muslins,
Needles, Pins, Ribbons, &c. &c.

AT ONE O'CLOCK, THAT CELEBRATED ENGLISH HORSE,
BLUCHER,

LEFT: *In the auction listed on this handbill, slaves were to be sold alongside household goods and food.*

ABOVE: *Slaves were transported from West Africa to North America, South America, and the Carribean Islands.*

his teeth. He's 40 years old, if he's a day," one witness overheard potential buyers saying. "So they knock this buck down for a thousand dollars. They calls the men 'bucks' and the women 'wenches.' "

The kidnapped Africans then endured the rigorous process of "breaking in," learning to be subservient, acquiring some pidgin English, and getting a new name. Many men and women, weakened from the arduous journey, did not survive their first contact with new diseases to reach their final destination in the American states.

LEFT: *An overseer, himself a slave, leads other slaves out to work in the fields on this plantation in 1834.*

RIGHT: *Slaves were watched constantly to ensure that they worked without rest or diversion. Once they returned from work after dark, there were still more personal chores to attend to before they were able to rest.*

PLANTATION LIFE

Abullhorn would sound at four in the morning to give the slaves 30 minutes warning to have breakfast and get out into the fields or up to the house. "Come the daybreak you hear the guinea fowls start potracking down at the edge of the woods lot," wrote ex-slave Charley Williams, remembering the mornings. "And then the roosters all start up round the barn, and the ducks finally wake up and join in. You can smell the old Sowbelly frying down at the cabins in the Row, to go with the hoecake and the buttermilk."

At noon the slaves received their allowance of cold bacon. Then they worked, worked, worked again until it was too dark to see. Then they performed more chores, personal ones this time, lit a fire, and ate supper in the cabin. Too soon, midnight came, and still they hadn't quite finished making a meal for lunch the next day.

"With a prayer that he might be on his feet and wide awake at the first sound of the horn," wrote Solomon Northup, a free black sold into slavery, describing the life of a slave, "he sinks to his slumbers nightly."

Slaves would have a food ration once a week of corn, bacon, or salt pork, supplemented with scraps of meat salvaged from the big-house kitchen or chickens stolen from the barn. Twice a year, they would get a clothing allowance, shoes every fall (in two sizes: adult and child), and a new blanket every third year.

"The principal food of those upon my master's plantation consisted of corn-meal and salt herrings," wrote Josiah Henson. "To which was added in summer a little buttermilk, and the few vegetables which each might raise for himself and his family, on the little piece of ground which was assigned to him for the purpose, called a truck-patch." Henson was born into slavery but escaped with his family in 1830 after 30 years of servitude. His memoirs, written when he was a freeman in Canada, are said to have been the inspiration for Harriet Beecher Stowe's *Uncle Tom's Cabin*.

If the working hours were long and the living conditions harsh, discipline was even harsher. Slaves who stepped out of line could expect a whipping or worse, from black drivers and white overseers as well as their white masters. Conditions did improve after 1808, when it became illegal to import new slaves. From this point on, slave owners were forced to care for their slaves, because buying new ones was more difficult. Even so, the slave population continued to grow, because any children born on the plantations were born into slavery.

ABOVE: *Josiah Henson's autobiography, published in 1839, was the inspiration behind the character of Uncle Tom in Harriet Beecher Stowe's novel.*

RIGHT: *On Sundays, their one day of rest, slaves were often permitted to play music and dance for their own pleasure.*

The slaves managed to hold on to African cultural rituals and to create new American ones, despite their continuing six-day-a-week ordeal. They adapted their culinary traditions to the foods they were able to find or grow for themselves; with artisanal skills, such as weaving and basketry, they provided household goods for themselves; they also found solace—and joy—in music and dance, singing while they worked and also for recreation. In fact, traditional African dances, brought across the Atlantic by people being transported to become slaves, are at the heart of many American popular dances, such as the shimmy or the Charleston. Other dances were performed for the entertainment of plantation owners. Good dancers could receive preferential treatment. Some dances incorporated an element of mockery in them: through their dance, slaves could make fun of their white masters. The cakewalk, for example, which later became popular on the vaudeville stage, began as a mockery of white pretension. The dance earned its name because some masters (oblivious of the fact that the joke was on them) organized cakewalk competitions among their slaves, with a cake as a prize. Even banjos were "brought hither from Africa," according to Thomas Jefferson in his *Notes on Virginia*. Drums were banned in case slaves used them to signal revolt, but the slaves developed alternative percussion instruments, using knees, spoons, or bones.

LEFT: *African Americans found relief from their harsh working conditions in music, singing, and dancing.*

SLAVE RELIGION

Religion was profoundly important in most slave communities. Many slaves held dearly to the beliefs they brought with them, combining them with Christian beliefs and practices taught to them by their masters to create a theology and practice that is at the root of many of today's African-American churches.

Some masters either required their slaves to attend church services or encouraged their slaves to hold their own services, hoping that Christian beliefs would make them more docile. However, the slaves borrowed only those elements of Christian teachings that offered them hope for the future, believing in a God who freed the Israelites from slavery rather than one who called for obedience to masters. The promise of freedom was strong—some of the leaders of slave rebellions, like Nat Turner, felt the call from God for armed insurrection. Other slave owners prohibited church services, fearful that any large gathering could breed rebellion—or not considering slave souls worthy of salvation. Practicing their own religion sometimes meant that slaves held secret services in the swamps or the woods. These followed distinctive patterns that imitated African rituals, such as call and response, " 'Thank God, I shall not live here always!' Then they pass from one to another, shaking hands, and bidding each other farewell, promising, should they meet no more on earth, to strive and meet in heaven, where all is joy, happiness and liberty," wrote one participant later. "As they separate, they sing a parting hymn of praise." These churches brought together communities and bonded extended families, united despite a law that refused to recognize family ties. Slaves developed their own marriage ceremonies based on half-forgotten rituals like jumping over a broom. Religious meetings were also a chance for free discussion. Additionally, preachers were highly respected and often leaders of their communities.

LEFT: *Under slavery, African Americans devised their own rituals, combining elements of Christianity with traditional African practices.*

RIGHT: *African-American churches prospered after slavery was abolished and then throughout the 20th century. This picture shows a baptism during a 1939 revival meeting in Virginia.*

FREE MEN

Throughout America's early history, there were always African Americans who lived as free men and women, in both the North and the South. The Massachusetts sailor Crispus Attucks was the first fatality of the American Revolution, and Peter Salem and Salem Poor fought in the Battle of Bunker Hill. These three were African Americans. In the northern colonies, many African Americans were freed when slavery was banned after the Revolution. Others were runaway slaves who succeeded in their escape. Still others managed, somehow, to purchase their freedom.

Although they were free, African Americans did not have equal rights with whites. Even in the North, segregation was the rule rather than the exception. Free blacks had to establish their own churches, schools, and businesses. The first black school

LEFT: *Free African Americans fought alongside white men in the American Revolution. This painting of the Boston Massacre shows Crispus Attucks as he is shot by British troops.*

opened in 1807, the first black college in 1842. The first patent to go to a black man was in 1834 when Henry Blair of Maryland invented a corn harvester. Work was hard to find. These were the days when the president of a mechanics' association in Cincinnati was prosecuted for helping a young black man learn a trade.

Making a stand

Many free African Americans actively campaigned against slavery and discrimination. Some were behind the Free Africa Petition of 1787 that demanded for blacks the same liberties that were laid out for whites in the Declaration of Independence. Others made their own stands. For instance, Benjamin Banneker, surveyor and astronomer, wrote angry letters accusing Thomas Jefferson of hypocrisy, and Massachusetts ship owner Paul Cuffe refused to pay taxes when he was barred from the ballot box in 1780.

LEFT: *This 1850s portrait depicts a prosperous freewoman. By holding an open book in her lap, she signals that she was able to read—a valuable achievement at a time when access to education was limited.*

SLAVE REVOLTS

Slaves in the South were not docile either. Some forms of protest were individual and subtle: working as slowly as possible, malingering. Others were more dramatic, ranging from escapes, both attempted and successful, to attempts to poison white masters. Throughout the period, slave owners and their families lived with horrible fears. They feared the burning of buildings and a sudden reversal of the power. They also feared that angry slaves would claim their freedom, inspired by the brilliant black general Toussaint L'Ouverture who freed the slaves of Haiti and by the propaganda of white abolitionists closer to home. Owners and overseers, as well as the local militia, were heavily armed, both to deter and to defend against attack. Any sign of conspiracy among slaves was met with harsh punishment, from whipping to death by public hanging.

However, these measures did not prevent attempts at large-scale rebellion. In 1800, one slave, named Gabriel Prosser, massed 1,000 slaves for an attack on Richmond, Virginia. However, a fierce rainstorm held them back before they could launch their offensive. The plot was revealed, and Prosser and 34 others were hanged. In 1822, Denmark Vesey, a free black, managed to organize thousands of slaves for a proposed attack on Charleston, South Carolina, but he was betrayed in advance.

White fears were realized in the bloody rebellion led by Nat Turner, a slave in Virginia. Turner began with only five coconspirators, but this small group attracted some 70 more to the cause. Together they killed 57 whites before their eventual defeat in Jerusalem, Virginia, where Turner was hanged in 1831. As he predicted, it rained after his execution.

LEFT: *After the slave revolt that he led was suppressed, Nat Turner managed to evade capture for six more weeks by hiding out in the woods.*

BELOW: *The majority of slave rebellions resulted in severe punishment—many who dared to revolt were hanged. For a few slaves, running away was the most successful means of revolt.*

JOHN JOSSELYN

Visiting Samuel Maverick from Massachusetts in 1639

"The second of October, about 9 of the clock in the morning, Mr Maverick's Negro woman came to my chamber window, and in her own Countrey language and tune sang very loud and shrill . . . whereupon I repaired to my host, to learn of him the cause, and intreat him in her behalf, to learn of him the cause [of her grief], for that I understood before, that she had been a Queen in her own Countrey, and observed a very humble and dutiful garb used towards her by another Negro who was her maid."

LIBERATION

Anderson was replying to a letter from his old owner, asking him to come "home." The former slave gently reminded the southern colonel that last time they met, the colonel had tried to shoot him. "Now, if you will write and say what wages you will give me, I will be better able to decide whether it would be to my advantage to move back again." History

> "I want to know particularly what the good chance is you propose to give me," reads an 1865 letter from Jourdon Anderson, a former slave from Tennessee. "I am doing tolerably well here; I get $25 a month, with victuals and clothing; have a comfortable home for Mandy (the folks here call her Mrs Anderson), and the children, Milly, Jane, and Grundy, go to school and are learning well; the teacher says Grundy has a head for a preacher. They go to Sunday School, and Mandy and me attend church regularly."

did not record what reply he received, if any, but Anderson stayed in Ohio.

Even so, the new respect, the hope, and the right to education and to church attendance were enough to demonstrate that another revolution had taken place in America. For a brief period, at least, life was going to be different for the four million slaves from the Old South.

RIGHT: *For many African Americans, liberation did not mean better living conditions—but hope for a better future.*

THE ABOLITION CAMPAIGN

The change was a long time coming. Debate over the legality and ethics of slave ownership had started well before the American Revolution. In the 1830s, though, the burning resentment of slaves and the free African Americans North and South turned into a protest movement that would eventually split the United States. The catalyst might have been the Nat Turner Uprising (*see page 22*), which triggered powerful feelings among both blacks and whites. Southern slave owners were more frightened for their lives than ever before and on the defensive against increasing anti-

ABOVE: *White abolitionists helped lead thousands of slaves to freedom along a secret route of safehouses and hiding places.*

RIGHT: *After her escape from slavery in 1849, Harriet Tubman risked her own life to lead other slaves along the Underground Railroad.*

slavery sentiment. Additionally, abolitionists were galvanized by the response to their work among slaves and their masters. The successes of the Underground Railroad buoyed abolitionists while simultaneously dismaying slave owners. Thousands of slaves each year escaped from the South. They took shelter in a secret network of hiding places and safe houses, and were guided part of the way by abolitionist "conductors." Harriet Tubman, herself an escaped slave, was one of the most successful conductors—she personally led around 300 slaves to freedom.

While many white people were committed to the abolitionist movement, the most powerful voices—and the lion's share of financial support—came from the black community. The Anti-Slavery Society was founded by black freemen in the North in the 1830s. Forceful black abolitionists were finding that they could make their voice heard in publications such as William Lloyd Garrison's *The Liberator*. During this period, abolitionists encouraged former slaves to record their memories of life under slavery for publication. These slave narratives, such as Harriet Jacobs's *Incidents in the Life of a Slave Girl* or Frederick Douglass's autobiography, movingly recounted the experiences of life in the slave system. They helped to sway many people to the abolitionist cause.

FREDERICK DOUGLASS

One of the most powerful orators of the age was born into slavery as Frederick Bailey. He escaped with the help of Anna Murray, a free black woman who would later become his wife, by borrowing a sailor suit in Baltimore in 1838. He did so using an official paper with an eagle on the top.

LEFT: *One of the many anthems of the abolitionist movement was written by lyricist Jesse Hutchinson and dedicated to Frederick Douglass.*

ABOVE: *With his resounding speaking voice, Frederick Douglass was an impassioned campaigner for abolition who swayed many to the cause.*

Douglass (the name he adopted once free) was an arresting figure: tall, with a mop of hair, a deep baritone voice, burning eyes, and an enormous forehead. Through his mimicry, he made people laugh at slave owners for their hypocrisy. His vivid descriptions of life in the South made his listeners feel what the slaves felt.

After a successful speaking tour of England and Ireland—he left the United States once his autobiography, entitled *Narrative of the Life of Frederick Douglas, An American Slave* (1845), gave away his whereabouts to his former master—he settled in Rochester, New York. Douglass then started publishing the abolitionist newspaper, *North Star*. (By the time of the Civil War, there were 40 other papers like it.) Douglass advocated equality for all people, black and white, men and women alike—he was one of the few male supporters of women's suffrage and was present at the famous Seneca Falls Convention.

Douglass was joined on the speaker's platform by some impressive black women—among them people like Maria Stewart, famous as the first black woman to speak in public, and the former slaves Harriet Tubman (*see page 25*) and Sojourner Truth. "Old woman," shouted one heckler at Sojourner Truth. "Do you think your talk about slavery does any good? Why, I don't care more for your talk than I do for the bite of a flea!"

"Perhaps not," she replied. "But the good Lord willing, I'll keep you scratching."

QUILTS

The few surviving quilts made by African American women under slavery are a powerful link to the past and the harbingers of a new tradition. The origins of the quilts are lost in time. However, we know the women must have had little time to sew for themselves and had to make use of what scraps they could rescue from the plantation houses, colored with vegetable dyes, to make bed coverings for their families.

These quilts, incorporating symbols of freedom such as Jacob's Ladder or the North Star, were potent images for the abolitionist movement. They were sold in the North to raise money for the cause. A quilt hung in front of a house sometimes signified that it was a safe house for escaping slaves.

The quilting tradition continued even after the Civil War, often out of economic necessity. As the twentieth century wore on, quilting increasingly became the preserve of older women. Only in recent years has quilt-making been adopted by a new generation of younger women.

MASON-DIXON LINE

40°N

Ohio

Pennsylvania

West Virginia

Virginia

Maryland

Delaware

LEFT: *The Mason-Dixon Line (the 40th Parallel) divided Union North from Confederate South in the Civil War.*

FAR RIGHT: *The 54th Massachusetts Volunteers arrived as vital reinforcements during the Battle of Olustee in 1864, saving the Union troops from disaster.*

BELOW: *The Guards of the 107th Colored Infantry proudly holding their muskets. Organized in Kentucky in 1864, they saw a lot of action over the following two years.*

THE CIVIL WAR

When the Civil War finally arrived, African Americans thronged to the army recruiting stations, hired drill halls, and prepared to fight to free the slaves. However, the government in Washington thanked them and asked them to return home. (However, free blacks were admitted to the navy—one in four sailors in the Union Navy were black, and shared the same quarters as whites.)

Thanks to the early military successes of the Confederate rebels, Lincoln's policy changed. From 1863, blacks were allowed to enlist in the army, usually in all-black regiments. By the end of the war, 165,000 blacks had served in the Union Army, and taken part in some of the most heroic charges of the Civil War. Many refused to accept any pay until it rose to the promised "equality" level of $13 a month. "Hurrah for Massachusetts and seven dollars a month," shouted the renowned 54th Massachusetts Volunteers, a black regiment, as they charged into the Battle of Olustee.

Some black women also played an important part in the Civil War. Harriet Tubman, for example, worked as a scout and organized slave intelligence networks behind enemy lines in the South. The involvement of African Americans almost certainly tipped the balance in favor of the Union side.

FREEDOM

In September 1862, President Abraham Lincoln issued the Emancipation Proclamation, mandating that all slaves in states in rebellion against the Union were free. It had little legal impact, though, since the southern, slave-owning states did not recognize the authority of the Union government. Even so, the Emancipation Proclamation was a clear statement of policy and made it apparent that Lincoln would in time abolish slavery. It was due to take effect on January 1, 1863.

That New Year's Eve, African Americans all over Union territory gathered in churches and halls to celebrate the dawning of a new era. On the islands off the coast of South Carolina, both races celebrated in the camp of the local Union volunteers. When the colonel rose and gathered his thoughts for a moment, an elderly African American in the audience began singing "My country 'tis of thee, sweet land of liberty." "I never saw anything so electric; it made all other words cheap," said the colonel, T. W. Higginson. "It seemed the choked voice of a race at last unloosed."

ABOVE RIGHT: *Although its value was mostly symbolic, the Emancipation Proclamation demonstrated Abraham Lincoln's commitment to the abolition of slavery.*

RIGHT: *Freedmen in the North rejoiced on January 1, 1863, the day on which the Emancipation Proclamation took effect. Northern blacks were the most active group of supporters for the abolitionist movement.*

LEFT: *During the Civil War, former slaves provided essential labor, supporting the Union cause in the cities as well as on the battlefields.*

B-400

RIGHT: *Harriet Tubman (far left) stands with a group of former slaves whom she led to freedom along the Underground Railroad. Until the Emancipation Proclamation took effect, freed slaves continued to fear discovery by their former masters.*

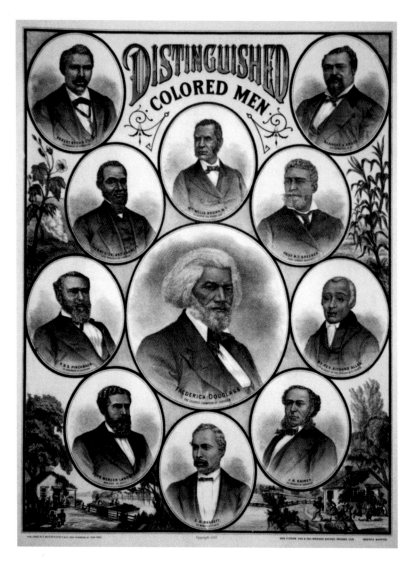

RIGHT: *Following the end of the Civil War, freed slaves made their way north in droves. This group is shown crossing the Confederate lines at Newbern, North Carolina.*

LEFT: *A nineteenth-century print showing "distinguished colored men." At center is Frederick Douglass, a leading campaigner for racial equality and the abolition of slavery.*

VICTORY

Following Confederate General Robert E. Lee's surrender in April 1865, news that the Union Army was victorious spread to plantations across the South. "Hallelujah broke out," said one witness, Felix Haywood. "Soldiers, all of a sudden, was everywhere—coming in bunches, crossing, walking and riding. Everyone was a-singing. We was all walking on golden clouds. Hallelujah!"

It was a period of unbridled hope. "Go out in any direction, and you meet Negroes on horses, Negroes on mules, Negroes with oxen, Negroes by the wagon, cart and buggy load," Presbyterian missionary Thomas Calahan reported from Louisiana. "Negroes on foot, men, women and children . . . Negroes in rags, Negroes in frame houses, Negroes living in tents, Negroes living in rail pens covered with brush, and Negroes living under brush piles without any rails, Negroes living on the bare ground with the sky for their covering; all hopeful,

almost all cheerful, everyone pleading to be taught, willing to do anything for learning." Millions began tilling the land they hoped would be distributed to them. The short-lived Bureau of Refugees, Freed Men, and Abandoned Lands (or the Freedmen's Bureau for short) was established to help freed slaves and poor, displaced whites. It handed out medical aid, provided food distribution, and set up schools and colleges. There was an overwhelming demand for books and new schools in every corner of the South.

Despite the first stirring of new forms of repression, it was a moment of optimism. Former slave Blanche Kelso represented Mississippi in the Senate. A black governor held office in Louisiana. There were black generals, judges, solicitors, superintendents of education, and state treasurers. The idea that the old plantations would be broken up to provide "40 acres and a mule" for freed slaves— an idea in the end rejected by Congress—seemed to hold out the prospect of independent living.

ABOVE: *In this classroom in the Primary School for Freedmen in Vicksburg, Mississippi, adults and children learned side by side.*

BELOW: *Freed African Americans continued to work for white landlords on cotton plantations, but this time as sharecroppers in return for a share of the harvest.*

EARNING A LIVING

Times were tough, too. "You can stay here if you want to, but I ain't goin' to give you nothing but your victuals and clothes enough to cover your hide, not a penny in money, do no nigger get from me," said the former owner of Ann Evans, near Mobile, Alabama, when Evans asked if she could stay. "So I up and said, 'Why boss, dey tells me dat since freedom we git a little change,' and he cursed me to all de low names he could think of and drove me out like a dog. I didn't know what to do, or where to go."

Evans asked a man who passed by to buy her some shoes and ended up marrying him for a place to live. There were hundreds of thousands like her—but those who could earn a little were able to

spend it for the first time. Often, when the new farmers came to town to sell their cotton—traditionally carrying two jugs with them for the day, one for molasses and the other for whiskey—they would be prey to wily shopkeepers who would try to get them drunk and steal their money.

"At noon the throng was greatest, and up to that time fresh wagon-loads of men, women, and children, were continually arriving," wrote William Brown, a freed slave describing the regular scene in Huntsville, Alabama. "They came not only in wagons, but on horses, and mules, and on foot. Their dress and general appearance were very dissimilar. Some were dressed in a queer looking garment made of pieces of old army blankets, a few were appareled in faded military overcoats, which were liberally supplied with patches of other material. The women, unlike their husbands and other male relations, were dressed in finery of every conceivable fashion. All of them were decked out with many-colored ribbons. They wore pinchbeck jewelry in large quantities."

After selling their wares, the women would wander around the shops. The men, though, would move on to the dining saloon, finishing the meal with pies, puddings, and preserves. For once, it looked like the foundations of a reasonable life, although the hope was not to last for very long.

ABOVE: *Against a backdrop of buildings destroyed in combat, newly freed African Americans ponder their future in a southern town.*

BELOW: *Freed slaves who remained in the South were often victimized by white men.*

HENRY HIGHLAND GARNET

"I was born in slavery, and have escaped, to tell you, and others, what the monster has done, and is still doing."

MIGRATION

The future black leader Booker T. Washington was traveling through a southern city when he heard some brick masons calling out to someone called the "governor," urging him to hurry with the bricks. "Several times I heard the command 'Hurry up, Governor!' " he wrote in his autobiography.

"My curiosity was aroused to such an extent that I made inquiry as to who the 'Governor' was, and soon found that he was a colored man who at one time had held the position of Lieutenant-Governor of his state."

However, the optimism of the first years of African Americans' freedom in the South, when everything seemed possible—when black judges, senators, and governors were elected and appointed—was extremely short-lived. The backlash by former slave owners, racists, politicians, and officials who wanted no compromise with former slaves, began almost as soon as the Confederate States started to recover spiritually and economically from the war.

RIGHT: *Booker T. Washington addresses a crowd at the dedication of a cotton seed mill in Mississippi.*

ABOVE: *During Reconstruction, freedmen were eager to exercise their right to vote, which was often denied to them by white polling officials.*

RIGHT: *Hostile white mobs attacked black homes and businesses in the South, angry at the progress achieved during Reconstruction.*

DISAPPOINTMENT

The Fifteenth Amendment laid down that voting "shall not be denied or abridged . . . on any account of race, color, or previous condition of servitude." In practice, however, a potent combination of intimidation and violence by conservative supporters of the Democratic Party began to sweep their Republican opponents from power, sometimes in armed assaults on state government buildings.

In case that did not work, African Americans were removed from the electoral registers if they had failed to pay a "poll tax" or if they failed to read or interpret a section of the state constitution—to the satisfaction of white polling officials, who were themselves subjected to the same intimidation. If anyone spoke out against the renewed tyranny, black and white alike across the South would hear a knock on the door in the night or receive a firebomb through the window, or worse.

With the emergence of the Ku Klux Klan came the constant fear of violence and the lynch mobs. Lynchings were the least of it. Men and women were burned alive, hacked to death—sometimes just for failing to call a white bully "mister." It was not unknown for the lynchings to be advertised in advance in newspapers so that crowds could come on chartered trains to watch.

"As far as the white man was concerned you were never to call him by his name," wrote North Carolina sharecropper Edgar Williams later. "You always said 'Mr.' or 'Mrs.' or 'Boss' or 'Captain.' People know them as Klan, but we called it Redneck. If we didn't call them Redneck we called them Paddy Rovers, because if a white man was near, somebody would say 'Paddy Rover coming,' the white man wouldn't know what you were speaking of, but the rest of blacks would know."

ABOVE LEFT: *This cartoon expresses the fear of violence experienced by many African-American families in the decades after the Civil War.*

LEFT: *African-American sharecroppers were at the mercy of landowners, who kept their tenant farmers in a form of financial bondage.*

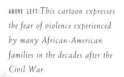

BELOW: *A cross-burning at a meeting of the Ku Klux Klan. The burning cross was a terrifying symbol of the KKK's violence toward African Americans and their supporters.*

RIGHT: *The Northeastern Federation of Colored Women's Clubs campaigned actively against lynching. This leaflet reported on a Congressional vote on an anti-lynching bill, which was passed by the House and was awaiting confirmation by the Senate.*

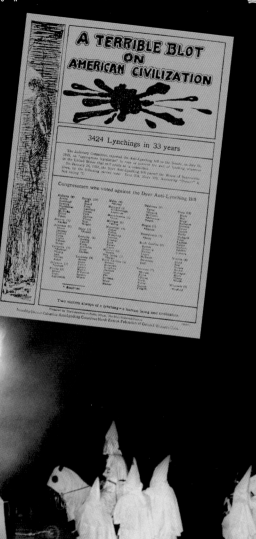

LEFT: *These cotton harvesters are waiting for the work day to begin on an Arkansas plantation. Many sharecroppers found it impossible to escape from spiraling into greater and greater debt.*

FINDING WORK

Many African Americans were free only in the narrowest possible sense. The "40 acres and a mule" the freedmen of the South had been expecting never materialized. For those who failed to find employment as domestic servants or factory workers, the economic future was bleak and looked remarkably like slavery.

Many worked as sharecroppers, growing cotton for a white landlord in return for a third or a half of the harvest. All too often, the books were kept by the white farmer, and the sharecroppers found themselves falling deeper and deeper into debt. "When we worked on shares, we couldn't make nothing—just overalls, and something to eat," said Henry Blake, a freed slave from Little Rock, Arkansas. "Half went to the white man, and you would destroy your half, if you weren't careful. A man that didn't know how to count would always lose. He might lose anyhow. The white folks didn't give no itemized statements. No, you just had to owe so much. No matter how good account you kept, you had to go by their account."

Sometimes African Americans would find that their debts had been paid off by a white farmer who agreed to let them work off the debt. By the end of the year, though, he had charged them so much for food and accommodations, that the debt was even higher than before. This system was known as peonage. It sank black families back into precisely the pattern of forced labor they had only just escaped.

Worse, Black Codes were passed by state governments to limit black civil rights and to regulate mobility and contact between the races. They were toughest in Mississippi. Every January, all blacks needed written proof of employment for the year ahead. There were fines for insulting whites or preaching without a license. In South Carolina, African Americans were hit by a punitive tax if they worked other than as farmers or domestic servants. Traveling performers or self-employed salespeople could be stopped by the police, accused of vagrancy and forced to work for free on the plantations.

Despite this tyranny, there were 25,000 black-owned businesses across the United States by the turn of the century. A quarter of the black farmers in the South were landowners by 1910.

RIGHT: *On this plantation outside of Dallas, Texas in 1907, children worked in the fields alongside their parents.*

Gathering Cotton on a Southern Plantation, Dallas, Texas.

BELOW: *Children attend to their lessons in this schoolroom in the Mississippi Delta. Many schools were organized by local African-American women's clubs.*

RIGHT: *A pastor preaches to his congregation in the African Church in Cincinnati, Ohio. African-American ministers were important community leaders.*

Blackie
Look at Blackie.
She is a good cow.
She give

SOUND FOUNDATIONS

Underlying the economic achievements of newly freed black men were the often unsung achievements of women, who held together extended families in the face of the struggle to survive. One of them was Elizabeth Johnson Harris, who described an upbringing in the 1870s in a two-story frame and brick building in Georgia specially built to rent to black people. Harris worked with her grandmother to keep the family running—fueled by her grandfather's ghost stories from the old days of slavery and by her grandmother's cooking.

"I would often sit patiently with her until one and two o'clock at night making quilt squares in small and large pieces," she wrote later. "She would cut the squares, and give me a certain lot or number even with hers—this kind of work we would do mostly on the long winter nights, dear old Grandpa would always have a comfortable fire."

The influence of black women was also apparent at a national level, due to the campaigns of such people as Ida Bell Wells-Barnett and the ambitious National Association of Colored Women. Additionally, other, smaller women's clubs sprang up all over the United States, representing the aspirations of an emerging black middle class. African-American women were often behind the successful organizations that launched new orphanages, schools, clinics, and hospitals, or opened homes for seniors. These women also often ran kindergartens, or campaigned for new playgrounds and for the closure of brothels.

The church also offered essential support. Former slave preachers like John Jasper and his Sixth Mount Zion Baptist Church, or trained black ministers like Benjamin Tucker Tanner of the First Colored Presbyterian Church in Washington, held their congregations together. These preachers offered their flocks spiritual and emotional guidance.

A source of support

Elizabeth Johnson Harris described Sundays that included anything up to six visits to church. "First, early morning prayer meetings, nine o'clock service, eleven o'clock service, three o'clock afternoon service, four o'clock service, and night service, then very frequently during the week, I had to attend these services by the orders or rules of my dear old grandmother, and also as company to be with her —yet I was mostly always willing and I believed I pleased the Lord and I know he has blessed me."

Black churches were at the roots of the network of black lodges, schools, and black colleges, and eventually black insurance companies and credit unions, that provided an infrastructure for African Americans. The churches were also the bastion against white power—demonstrating to their followers that African Americans had standing, and constantly reminding young blacks about who they were and what they could be.

JIM CROW

"Every time I wheel about/I jump Jim Crow," sang Thomas Dartmouth Rice in the 1840s, a white entertainer who "blacked up" to sing and dance in one of the minstrel acts popular from the turn of the century onward. By the end of the century, though, "Jim Crow" had a much darker meaning, as the general name for state regulations that segregated the races. These were endorsed by the 1896 U.S. Supreme Court decision *Plessy v. Ferguson*, which stated that segregation was constitutional.

All public facilities were segregated and definitely not equal. The so-called Jim Crow railroad carriages were obviously below standard. Forcing blacks to sit at the back of buses was humiliating. In Oklahoma—where African Americans had hoped to found a black state—there were separate telephone booths. In Atlanta, there were even separate Bibles to swear on in the courthouse. Blacks had to be off the streets by 10:00 p.m. in Mobile, Alabama. No redress was available.

The last African-American congressman for 70 years, George H. White, resigned from the House of Representatives sadly in 1901 and moved to New Jersey. "I can no longer live in North Carolina and be a man," he said. Thousands of others were searching for ways of making the same journey.

RIGHT (INSET): *African-American men wearing tuxedos demonstrate against "Jim Crow" segregation laws in 1944.*

BELOW: *Forced out of their homes by their landlords in Missouri, sharecroppers stand with their belongings on the road north.*

RIGHT: *Northern black neighborhoods like Harlem were a magnet for the discouraged and dispossessed people of the southern states.*

THE GREAT MIGRATION

These were difficult times for farmers, with a depressed economy, constant Mississippi floods, and the arrival of the boll weevil pest. At the same time, racial violence was at its peak, and official discrimination created an unbreakable barrier. Slowly but surely, black southerners began to make the journey in search of work to the big cities of the North—New York, Philadelphia, and Chicago. By 1915, this trickle had become a flood—almost a third of a million people during World War I, ending up in the new ghettos around the factories in the north and west. Tenant farmers usually had to slip away under the cover of darkness. Train stations were guarded, and African Americans found on trains were sent back to their plantations. To escape, sharecroppers would walk ten or 20 miles to catch a train in another town.

Once they arrived, life was often no easier. White unions did not welcome black workers. White mobs sometimes roamed the streets. Although zoning on racial lines was illegal, all the cities soon developed invisible lines—enforced by landlords or mobs—between the white neighborhoods and the new black ghettos—Harlem, Watts, Paradise Valley, and North Philadelphia.

SPREADING THE CULTURE

African Americans crowded into Chicago's South Side and other suburbs, bringing with them the spirituals, the banjos and rhythms, and a new musical sound known as the blues (see page 73) that echoed the despair of the South. Many started work as bootblacks, ran restaurants, barbershops, and pool rooms. Some even entered real estate: Jesse Binga's "Binga Block" at 47th and State Streets was known as the longest tenement row in Chicago. Other African Americans worked as cooks in private homes, shops, restaurants, schools, hotels, and colleges. Black cooks, chefs, and waiters also worked in the Pullman cars of the old railroads and on the river steamboats.

Late migrants, moving north to join family members or friends, had an easier time of it. They were drawn there after reading battered copies of the *Chicago Defender* left by black Pullman porters working the trains south from Chicago. The *Defender* ran lists of rules on how to live in the city: don't go outside wearing an apron, don't laugh too loudly or "display hilarity." New arrivals were soon listening to radio broadcasts by Earl Hines and others from Chicago's Regal Ballroom. "Goin' to Chicago was like goin' out of the world," sang bluesman Muddy Waters.

FAR LEFT: *This barbershop in Oxford, North Carolina, tries to associate itself with the glamour of Harlem.*

LEFT: *A newsboy sells the* Chicago Defender, *one of the leading African-American newspapers.*

ABOVE: *The Earl Hines Grand Terrace Band was the sound of black Chicago in the 1920s. Hines himself stands in the front row, holding a newspaper.*

SOUL FOOD

The smell of sweet potatoes, corn, yams, pork, cabbage, cowpeas, and hoecakes cooking in big black pots over open fires pervaded the southern plantations. Recipes passed by word of mouth from plantation to plantation, merging with Native-American techniques for cooking local plants, such as hominy grits or pumpkin pie. Slaves had to be resourceful since their rations were always meager. They used the scraps of meat their masters would not eat—such as the small intestines (chitterlings) or thighs (hocks). They also stretched their meals by preparing starchy foods, like yams, corn, or rice, as they did in Africa.

Meanwhile, most well-to-do families, white and black, North and South, had African-American cooks. These wealthy people soon found themselves eating the same foods as their cooks' families. Black families ate hoecakes and molasses at breakfast, and these were also served to the well-to-do people. It was here—in the kitchens presided over by African-American women—that African traditions first influenced American food.

As African Americans migrated north to the industrial cities or west to the cattle drives, they took their recipes with them. African

Americans used whatever came to hand and adapted the recipes to local ingredients, spreading their tastes and techniques. Wherever you find candied yams, fried chicken, cornbread, or black-eyed peas—or the dishes developed to serve the customers of black restaurants in Hastings Street, Detroit, or Chicago's South Side, like baked ham or baked spaghetti—you know you are in the presence of African-American history.

RECIPE FOR HOECAKES

1 cup white cornmeal
½ teaspoon salt
¼ cup boiling water
2 teaspoons bacon fat, butter, or vegetable oil

Mix cornmeal and salt in bowl. Add boiling water, stirring constantly. Beat until smooth. Heat oil in a skillet. Put tablespoonfuls of the dough into the hot oil, and spread to form flat circles. Cook for two minutes on each side until golden brown, turning once. Dry on paper towels. Serve hot.

CIVIL RIGHTS

In 1901, Booker T. Washington—the pioneering educator and African-American leader—sat down to lunch at the White House with President Theodore Roosevelt. Never before had a black leader been invited to dine with the first family in the nation's capital.

It was a crucial moment in African-American history. The Jim Crow segregation laws were at their height across the South. Lynchings were taking place weekly, apparently with the connivance of the authorities. An unpleasant pseudo-scientific racism provided a license for leading "experts" to state and restate what they regarded as the "hopeless inferiority" of the African race.

Many African Americans resented Washington for dining with Roosevelt, who was unwilling to take any real steps toward improving conditions for African Americans. When Washington asked the president to intervene to stop lynchings, Roosevelt ignored him. When Washington urged him to intervene to help the so-called Brownsville Rioters—167 black soldiers discharged without honor after a shooting incident despite their credible claims of innocence—Roosevelt ignored him again.

Some felt that Washington's approach to the civil rights issue was too tame. He discouraged talk about civil rights, accepted segregation, and

RIGHT: *Written by leading social-rights campaigner Ida Bell Wells-Barnett (see page 43), this 1899 pamphlet campaigned against lynching and violence against blacks.*

Lynch Law in Georgia.

BY

IDA B. WELLS-BARNETT

A Six-Weeks' Record in the Center of Southern Civilization, As Faithfully Chronicled by the "Atlanta Journal" and the "Atlanta Constitution."

ALSO THE FULL REPORT OF LOUIS P. LE VIN.

The Chicago Detective Sent to Investigate the Burning of Samuel Hose, the Torture and Hanging of Elijah Strickland, the Colored Preacher, and the Lynching of Nine Men for Alleged Arson.

This Pamphlet is Circulated by Chicago Colored Citizens. 2939 Princeton Avenue, Chicago.

wanted African Americans to "earn" equality by making economic progress. His program, set out in a speech in Atlanta in 1895, became known as the Atlanta Compromise. "In all things that are purely social, we can be as separate as the fingers," he said, "yet one as the hand in all things essential to mutual progress." For many African Americans, though, Washington was a hero who provided a practical way forward that made sense from their position as domestic servants, small farmers, and unemployed migrants. Politicians respected and understood him, and he advised Presidents McKinley, Roosevelt, and Taft.

EQUALITY

EXERCISING THE RIGHT OF PETITION.

PASS THE
DYER BILL

DOWN WITH
LYNCHING

LYNCHING
MUST GO

A SILENT PARADE

Vote Against Those Who Voted
To Protect The Lynching Industry.

EXERCISING THE RIGHT OF SUFFRAGE.

VOTING
BOOTH

Join This Silent Parade

ABOVE: *Booker T. Washington*
dined with President Theodore
Roosevelt in October 1901. This
was the first time an African-
American leader was invited to
eat in the White House.

RIGHT: *This cartoon encouraged*
African Americans to protest
against lynchings, by public
demonstrations or by voting
against politicians who were in
favor of lynching.

RIGHT: *Students at the Tuskegee Institute in 1914 learning marketable skills by working with machines in the Institute's electrical division.*

BELOW: *Both men and women received training at the Tuskegee Institute. Here, women learn how to make mattresses.*

A CORNER IN THE ELECTRICAL DIVISION.

Washington was born into slavery in Virginia and was liberated by Union troops just before the end of the Civil War. After working his way through school and college, Washington rose to prominence as the founding principal of the Tuskegee Institute in Alabama, established by the state legislature as a school for blacks. His first classes there were held in an outbuilding owned by a black church, with a student holding an umbrella over him to keep off the rain leaking in from the roof. In 1882, donations from wealthy white philanthropists in the North allowed him to buy an old plantation, and he led the students in cleaning out the stable and henhouse. Obsessed with cleanliness and jealous of rivals with alternative tactics, Washington's plan was to teach artisan skills, to turn out good farmers and domestic servants. Tuskegee was enormously successful, but it was not enough for many African Americans.

ABOVE: *W. E. B. DuBois was a teacher, writer, and a tireless radical campaigner for civil rights.*

THE NIAGARA MOVEMENT

By the turn of the century, many blacks felt that Washington's prescription—keep your head down and get an education—needed another dimension. They began to unite around his increasingly influential rival W. E. B. (William Edward Burghardt) DuBois.

DuBois was a northern academic. He was born free and earned a Ph.D. from Harvard. He was a sociology professor, poet, novelist, and brilliant polemicist. In his speeches and his writings (notably his 1903 book *The Souls of Black Folk*), DuBois railed against segregation and inequality. In July 1905, he invited 28 black leaders—but not Washington—to a hotel in Buffalo. There they launched the Niagara Movement, a radical organization dedicated to ending segregation. Although the Movement was short-lived, it sowed the seeds for the foundation of the most famous African-American organization of the century, the National Association for the Advancement of Colored People. The NAACP was dedicated to making "11,000,000 Americans physically free from peonage, mentally free from ignorance, politically free from disenchantment, and socially free from insult." DuBois edited the NAACP's magazine, *The Crisis*, from 1910 to 1934, publishing the work of many great African-American writers and using its editorials to insist on equality in all areas of life.

DuBois lived to be 94 and to see the flowerings of the civil rights movement under Martin Luther King Jr. in the 1960s. All his life, he was a teacher and an activist. As he got older his focus broadened and he fought against imperialism all over the world. He emigrated to Ghana in 1961, and died there later that year.

THE GREAT DIVISION

The schism between the pragmatists and idealists, between the followers of Washington and DuBois, has remained ever since. It "marked a split of the race into two well-defined parties," wrote the black intellectual and artist James Weldon Johnson, then working at the State Department. Johnson, who also served as field secretary to the NAACP, made one contribution to unity by writing "Lift Every Voice and Sing," tears streaming down his face as he did so. The song (*left*) was adopted by the NAACP as the "Negro National Anthem."

> *"God of our weary years,*
> *God of our silent tears,*
> *Thou who has brought us thus far on our way;*
> *Thou who hast by thy might*
> *Led us into the light*
> *Keep us forever in thy path, we pray."*

Successful protest movements require both pragmatists and idealists, like Washington and DuBois. They also require the active interest of the people for whom they are fought. Most African Americans watched the progress of the campaign through black newspapers like the *Pittsburgh Courier* or the *Baltimore African-American*. On a grassroots level, there was a great deal of activity. African-American health and social organizations were established, and churches carried the word to black communities.

Ordinary lives were affected by everyday injustice. The vast majority of black children were in segregated schools. Only one in five southern blacks was registered to vote—the rest excluded by their failure to answer meaningless questions from officials like, "How many bubbles in a bar of soap?" Most were unable to buy a hot dog at a lunch counter. If they were served in a white drugstore, they would have their ice cream handed through a side window in a paper cup. They had to sit at the back in theaters and buses. At the end of the working day, African Americans had to struggle home on inadequate transport to all-black neighborhoods.

LEFT: *Shown here is the first issue of* The Crisis, *the monthly magazine of the NAACP which was published in November 1910 under the editorship of W. E. B. DuBois.*

LEFT: *Delegates at an annual meeting of the NAACP in Cleveland, Ohio. Since its foundation in 1910, it has grown into one of the most influential African-American advocacy groups.*

RIGHT: *Until the Civil Rights Act of 1964, public transportation was segregated and African Americans were required to sit in the rear of buses or in designated train carriages.*

BELOW: *On his way to a rally at Madison Square Garden in New York City in 1922, Marcus Garvey wore his uniform as self-proclaimed Provisional President of Africa.*

THE EXTREMISTS

Protest movements also require extremists—like the Jamaican-born African nationalist Marcus Garvey. During the 1920s, he was a hugely influential black leader, thrilling his audiences with his dreams of an African empire and the Black Star shipping line, which would help them to be repatriated.

"Up, you mighty race," proclaimed Garvey, a powerful speaker. "You can accomplish what you will." He rejected integration and maintained that no real progress could be made as long as African Americans were in the minority. Rather than working toward economic or political progress in the United States, he called for a return to Africa and the founding of an independent black state.

Millions of African Americans saw Garvey parade through the streets of New York in August 1920, wearing a cocked hat and a splendid uniform, as the self-proclaimed "Provisional President of Africa." He was followed by African Legionnaires in blue and red uniforms, Black Star nurses, the Black Eagle Flying Corps, the African Motor Corps, and his swirling red, black, and green flags. The audience listened to radical speeches, which condemned almost every other black leader for compromise with capitalism.

RIGHT: *During the boom years of the 1920s, both men and women ran highly successful African-American business ventures.*

Garvey's career was cut short by a 1925 conviction for mail fraud after he misused funds raised to start the Black Star Line. He was imprisoned and deported to Jamaica, where he died in obscurity.

THE BUSINESSPEOPLE

Despite Garvey's fervent oratory, the anti-capitalist message did not sway the hearts of most African Americans. Inspired by new black leaders and buoyed by the boom years of the 1920s, more people entered into business than ever before. "Negro businessmen talked about million dollar corporations as if they were playthings," wrote Vishnu Oak in *The Negro's Adventure in General Business* (1949), "and started corporate enterprises for the production of articles of every description, including brooms, dolls, mayonnaise, perfume and toilet goods, hair preparations, hosiery, cotton, and woolen goods, mattresses, flour, chemicals, dyes, radios, movies, lumber, burial caskets, tiles, coal, oil, and stoves."

The prosperity could not last. The Wall Street Crash came, and African Americans were hit harder by the Depression than anyone else. Fortunately, many could fall back on churches and mutual aid societies, as well as the "underground" economy, organizing chicken dinners, selling homebrew, or running house rent parties, just as they did in the early days of the migration northward.

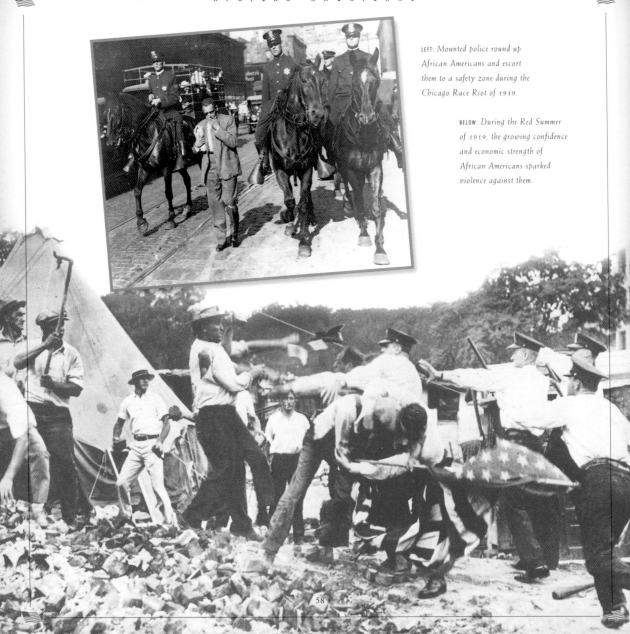

LEFT: *Mounted police round up African Americans and escort them to a safety zone during the Chicago Race Riot of 1919.*

BELOW: *During the Red Summer of 1919, the growing confidence and economic strength of African Americans sparked violence against them.*

THE WAR YEARS

"Can you go into a restaurant where white people dine? Can you get a seat in the theater where white people sit?" Those were two of the questions posed by a German propaganda leaflet dropped to American troops on the Western Front in World War I. The Germans believed that the Americans were vulnerable on the race issue—and they were.

The war forced the issue. It generated jobs in the northern cities and accelerated the great migration from the South. It gave black people a glimpse of freedom: Europe was obviously a more tolerant place than home. African Americans returned from World War I with greater self-confidence and determined to make changes.

"We return fighting, having fought for democracy in Europe," wrote W. E. B. DuBois in 1919. "We are cowards and jackasses if . . . we do not marshal every ounce of our brain and brawn to fight a sterner, longer, more unbending battle against the forces of hell in our own land."

This positive outlook, however, was short-lived. Increased African-American confidence unleashed a violent backlash in 1919 known as the Red Summer, which left scores of blacks dead across the nation. One African American

RIGHT: *In 1941, this group of African Americans enlisted in the United States Army Air Corps. It was the first time African Americans were allowed in this branch of the military.*

was lynched in his southern hometown just for walking around wearing his uniform.

A generation later, the same kind of rising optimism occurred after Pearl Harbor. The rhetoric of freedom and equality trotted out by the Allies was easily adapted to portray the cause of African Americans back home. "We must overthrow Hitlerism within as well as Hitlerism without," proclaimed the NAACP paper *The Crisis*. As the African-American pianist John Malachi put it, "I felt like if I was going into the military, I should've been going down to Mississippi to fight somebody down there."

African Americans had already received a boost in federal aid as a result of President Franklin Delano Roosevelt's New Deal, designed to beat the Depression. This included projects to collect the

songs and memories of former slaves. By following advice from his generals, Roosevelt began World War II by refusing to integrate the armed forces. A proposed march on Washington, D.C. threatened to bring the city to a standstill, and Roosevelt allowed his bluff to be called.

African Americans fought bravely in every theater of war. There was the first black Air Corps unit, the 99th Pursuit Squadron. There was even the first black general, Benjamin O. Davis Sr. At the same time, U.S. government propaganda celebrated the melting pot at home and enforced mixed workforces in industry, despite sometimes violent strikes by white workers.

Once again, the war opened people's eyes to injustice. Northern black soldiers were enraged by their treatment in the South. They were astonished to discover, when they were posted to England, that their own white officers were discouraging friendly locals from "fraternizing" with them.

By 1945, it was clear that African Americans were increasingly prepared to challenge the status quo. Nearly half a million were members of the NAACP. The U.S. president, now Harry S. Truman, was motivated to set up a President's Committee on Civil Rights.

LEFT: *These men were some of the first graduating African-American U.S. Army Air Corps Pilots, based at the Advanced Flying School in Tuskegee, Alabama.*

RIGHT: *Before embarking for Europe, men of the all-black Unit 4505-C of the 780th MP battalion pose proudly. The unit was commanded by a white officer.*

CIVIL RIGHTS HEROES

Most African Americans were not members of the NAACP, however, preferring to keep their heads down and their families safe. Many victims of racial violence were ordinary people. Emmett Till, a 14-year-old from Chicago, was murdered in Mississippi for saying "Bye, baby" to a white store owner's wife. Reverends George W. Lee and Lamar Smith were both murdered for refusing to take their names off voter registration lists in the same state. Four children attending Sunday school died during a bomb attack on the Sixteenth Street Baptist Church in Birmingham, Alabama, 18 days after Martin Luther King Jr.'s "I have a dream" speech. Most certainly never took part in the marches and boycotts of the 1950s and 1960s, and many actively disapproved of them.

Everyone, though, celebrated the great moments in the battle for civil rights. These included the time when Eleanor Roosevelt—wife President F.D.R. and a tireless equality campaigner—deliberately sat between black and white delegates in a mixed-race campaign meeting in Birmingham, Alabama, in 1938, in defiance of the racist local police chief, Eugene "Bull" Connor.

Another example was when the veteran black lawyer Thurgood Marshall rubbed his hands with glee as he realized that the state of Texas had made it possible to get the Supreme Court to rule on segregation. "We got these boys!" he exclaimed

—and indeed they had. The court banned segregated universities and went on to ban segregated dining cars.

Another rallying point involved Rosa Parks, a seamstress in a department store in Montgomery, Alabama. While on her way home by bus after a tiring day at work in 1955, she was ordered to move because of local laws that ruled that no black could sit parallel to a white person. Her courageous refusal and her later arrest led to the Montgomery Bus Boycott the following year, which marked the real beginning of the civil rights movement.

An additional great moment involved Melba Pattillo. This student was determined to enforce her right—granted under the Supreme Court decision *Brown v. Board of Education* (1954)—to go to Central High School in Little Rock, Arkansas, in 1957. She was assaulted by a white man shouting, "I'll show you niggers the Supreme Court cannot run my life." The ensuing disorder forced the hand of President Dwight D. Eisenhower, who sent in the 101st Airborne Division troops to protect the African-American children.

Another example involved four students in Greensboro, North Carolina. Their sit-in protest at the lunch counter at Woolworth's—during which they were punched, burned with cigarettes, and covered in ketchup—sparked off a wave of sit-ins in supermarkets, libraries, and chain stores all over the South. These involved 70,000 students and led to 3,600 arrests.

Of course, no one could forget Martin Luther King Jr. himself. He wrote an inspirational "Letter from Birmingham City Jail" on prison toilet paper. He had been arrested by "Bull" Connor during the Birmingham, Alabama, demonstrations, along with hundreds of children as young as six, in one of the great set piece civil rights trials of strength.

LEFT: *On December 21, 1956—the day a Supreme Court ruling desegregated public buses in Montgomery, Alabama—Rosa Parks sits in the front of a city bus. Her refusal to move to the back of the bus the previous year inspired the Montgomery bus boycott.*

RIGHT: *African-American students being protected by the army as they leave Little Rock Central High School in 1957. At a demonstration earlier that day, a black student was burned in effigy.*

MARTIN LUTHER KING JR.

" I have earnestly worked and preached against violent tension, but there is a type of constructive non-violent tension that is necessary for growth," wrote King. It was the cornerstone of his belief in non-violence, inspired by the liberation teachings of the black churches and by tactics pioneered by Mahatma Gandhi against the British in India.

Brilliant and inspirational, King was dogged by the FBI, pursued by allegations about his private life, guilt-ridden about his own family, and exhausted by internecine brawling inside the movement. King, though, gave the campaign a focus, helping to make it a recognizable, sympathetic cause on television screens all over the world.

This personal journey culminated in the crowd of a quarter of a million—a quarter of them white—that marched on Washington, D.C. in 1963 to hear his speech about a dream that was to become one of the most famous in a century of famous speeches. President Lyndon B. Johnson responded with his War on Poverty, the Civil Rights Act of 1964, and the Voting Rights Act the following year. One did away with segregation; the other ushered in the age of a black electorate. All, however, came far too late to avoid a legacy of bitterness.

ABOVE: *Martin Luther King Jr. was one of the most charismatic and effective spokesmen for civil rights. His assassination in April 1968 stunned the nation.*

RIGHT: *King acknowledges the immense crowds gathered at the Lincoln Memorial for the March on Washington on August 28, 1963.*

"I say to you today, my friends, so even though we face the difficulties of today and tomorrow, I still have a dream," he declared. "It is a dream deeply rooted in the American dream. I have a dream that one day this nation will live out the true meaning of its creed—we hold these truths to be self-evident, that all men are created equal."

RIOTS AND BLACK POWER

Starting in the mid-1960s, a new breed of black activist, the Black Power Movement, claimed much limelight and rejected non-violence. King himself turned his energies toward the fight against poverty. His work was bought to a tragic end in Memphis on April 17, 1968, when he was felled by a sniper's bullet. "We now have the type of black man on the scene in America today . . . who just doesn't intend to turn the other cheek any longer." That was how Malcolm X warned of future relations between the races in a speech to the Cory Methodist Church in Cleveland, Ohio, in 1964. The following year, he was dead—shot by two former Black Muslims.

Malcolm X was right. The mid-1960s were already too late to avoid serious trouble. His own death came a few months before six days of rioting in Watts, in Los Angeles. More than 30 African Americans were killed in the riots, which also caused more than $45 million of damage.

The trigger had been the arrest of African-American teenager Marquette Frye for driving while intoxicated, and the subsequent police manhandling of his mother. Rioters singled out white-owned businesses that they believed had been exploiting the black community. "The mood of Watts last week smacked less of defeat than victory and power," wrote *Newsweek*. The 1967 race riots in Newark, New York, Buffalo, New Haven, Milwaukee, Atlanta, Boston, and, worst of all, Detroit left hundreds more dead. It was the era of Black Power and Huey P. Newton and Bobby Seale's Black Panthers. They wore black berets and dark glasses, shadowing the police on their patrols in Oakland, California.

It also saw the emergence of the Nation of Islam as a serious political force. Since Mohammed Alexander Webb proclaimed himself a Muslim at the World's Columbian Exposition in Chicago in 1893, a steady stream of African Americans had followed the same path—answering an ancestral memory of a Muslim rather than a Christian faith. In 1930, the mysterious Wallace D. Fard appeared in Detroit, Michigan, preaching black nationalism, economic self-sufficiency, discipline, and a creed combining elements of Islam, Christianity, and spiritualism. Fard founded the Nation of Islam there in the same year. Subsequent leaders—Elijah Mohammed, Malcolm X, Louis Farrakhan, and others—have led the Nation of Islam from strength to strength.

> ### R. S. COLLINGWOOD
>
> A Black Man's Appeal to his White Brothers.
>
> *"I went to a station to purchase my ticket. I was there 30 minutes before the ticket office was opened. When the ticket office opened, I at once appeared at the window. While the agent served the white people at the other side I remained there beating the window until the train pulled out. I was compelled to jump on the train without my ticket and wire back to have my trunk expressed."*

LEFT: *A convert to Islam, the black nationalist leader Malcolm X came to believe that separatism was not essential for African-American progress.*

RIGHT: *Pupils and teachers in Fillmore, San Francisco voice their support of the Black Panthers outside a "liberation school" in 1969.*

AFRICAN-AMERICAN MUSIC

The former slave Solomon Northup remembered the Christmas dances as the one bright spot of his years in chains—and as "genuine happiness, rampant and unrestrained." "Go down to Louisiana," he urged, "and see the slaves dancing in the starlight of a Christmas night."

Before the "Black Swan," when Elizabeth Taylor Greenfield dazzled Queen Victoria with her

BELOW: *At a Christmas dance on a southern plantation, African Americans rejoice in singing and dancing.*

> **SOLOMON NORTHUP**
>
> *"Had it not been for my beloved banjo, I scarcely can conceive how I could have endured the long years of bondage."*

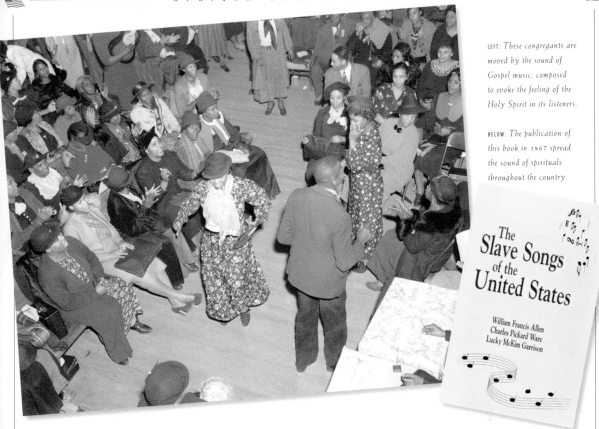

The
Slave Songs
of the
United States

William Francis Allen
Charles Pickard Ware
Lucky McKim Garrison

extraordinary voice; before the sounds of the spiritual (W. E. B. DuBois called them "sorrow songs") were heard throughout the country; before black minstrel troupes were expected to "black up" with burned cork when on stage just like white minstrel acts did—before all this, there were clear signs of the nascent African-American influence on music and dance.

One of those was Congo Square in New Orleans, Louisiana, where the city council had confined "assemblies of slaves" from 1817. This regulation had been intended as a way of controlling potentially dangerous gatherings. However, the rhythms, the singing, and the captivating dancing by African Americans and Jamaicans turned Congo Square into a major tourist attraction for more than 60 years.

FROM RELIGION TO RAGTIME

Under the yoke of slavery, African Americans expressed themselves creatively through song and dance. On Sundays, the one day that offered respite from hard labor, spirituals that poetically recounted biblical stories shaped their worship. These spirituals, with their religious roots and hidden messages of liberation, became popular among both blacks and whites after the Civil War with the publication of *Slave Songs of the United States* in 1867. Soon enough, the Great Migration (*see pages 36–49*) brought spirituals out of the South and into the big northern cities, where they were quickly taken up by the new Pentecostal or Holiness churches. Traditional spirituals were also at the heart of a new style of music—gospel music. Their lyrics recounted personal responses to God, to religion, and to life. Their stirring use of instrumentals was said to sound like the arrival of the Divine. Gospel music reaches into the hearts of its listeners, drawing them into the emotions

BELOW: *A choir in a Detroit church singing gospel music. Some songs, such as "Let my People Go," have become international anthems of resistance.*

of the song and inviting them to sing along. Many of these songs, with their not-so-distant memory of slavery—songs like "Swing Low, Sweet Chariot" and "Let My People Go"—have become international anthems of resistance in the face of oppression.

Not all African-American music, though, was devotional. On the plantations, slaves sang and danced for fun as well as for salvation. Some white masters viewed this personal expression as dangerous and tried to curtail it. Others enjoyed it and made their slaves dance and sing for them.

A tradition also arose of minstrel shows, popular entertainment in which white comic performers "blacked up" and sang and danced in ridiculous imitation of the supposed manners of black people. While most minstrel troupes consisted of white comics, there were some notable black performers. One example is the Georgia Minstrels, founded by George B. Hicks in 1865, which toured the United States for 30 years. At its peak, the Georgia Minstrels employed 21 black performers and two of the most brilliant banjo players in the world, Billie Kersands and Sam Lucas.

RIGHT: *In many minstrel shows, such as John R. Van Arnam's touring troupe, white performers "blacked up" to do their routines.*

Lucas went on to launch the Creole Show in 1891. This introduced a new style of black musical comedy, including beautiful dancing women, that put African-American talent onto the vaudeville stage on its own terms. Another Georgia Minstrel was James Bland, who heard former slaves singing while he was at law school. He dropped out to become a banjo player and composer. He wrote "Carry Me Back to Old Virginny," which became Virginia's official state song in 1940, "Oh, Dem Golden Slippers," and "There's a Long, Long Trail a Winding," which would soon be sung by European armies on their way to the Western Front.

This was also the era of ragtime, another distinctively African-American contribution. With its lively, syncopated rhythms, ragtime is made for dancing. It emerged from the jooks—black music bars—of the Old South. It culminated in Scott Joplin's "Maple Leaf Rag" (1899), which sold more than one million copies in sheet music alone.

Joplin and colleague Otis Saunders began their careers playing in piano bars across Oklahoma. The new sound spread quickly once white music publishers, always on the lookout for the next new trend, discovered it. Ragtime's greatest triumph took place in May 1912, when as many as 125 black musicians of the Clef Club Orchestra played a massive concert in New York's Carnegie Hall. They would be the first of many African-American musicians to make their way there.

BELOW: *W. C. Handy, famous as the composer of St. Louis Blues, is credited with creating the Memphis Blues sound.*

BLUES

Nobody knows who first started singing the blues. It emerged out of the disappointments of freedom and the poverty of sharecropping in the Mississippi Delta around the turn of the century. Sung by men with a guitar rather than a banjo, the blues owes its haunting, sad sound to the use of slightly flattened notes—and to the sentiment behind it.

"The thing of it is, is women and men ain't always going to get along," said John Ruskie of the Delta Blues Museum, explaining why the blues will always exist. This was a form of musical expression that could cover the pain of love as well as the pain of work.

One of the men who helped to define the blues was the African-American composer W. C. Handy. Handy grew up in Alabama, hearing spirituals. He was working as director of a black band in Tutwiler, Mississippi, in 1903 when he first heard the sound of the blues. He became an immediate convert and eventually composed the quintessential 12-bar blues song "St. Louis Blues."

BESSIE SMITH AND BILLIE HOLIDAY

During the 1920s, blues recordings spread the African-American sound further and wider. Through the influence of record labels, female vocalists, backed by big bands, came to the fore. Bessie Smith is one of those women. She remains one of the greatest blues singers of all time. After joining Ma Rainey's troupe, the Rabbit Foot Minstrels, when she was just 11, Smith rose to became one of the highest-paid singers in the United States. She was famous for "Nobody Knows You When You're Down and Out" and for atmospheric lines redolent of the South like "Back in Black Mountain, I sure would smack your face/ Children cryin' for liquor and all the birds sing bass."

Bessie Smith's life and career were tragically cut short by an automobile accident in 1937. The blueswoman baton was handed on to Billie Holiday. Holiday struggled against drug addiction and the scars of her upbringing. In the great tradition of the blues, she used that pain to interpret familiar blues songs in whole new directions.

Holiday began singing for 10 dollars a week in the late 1920s in New York City clubs. From 1933, she linked up with the great jazz bands of Louis Armstrong, Duke Ellington, and others. Over the next 10 years, she recorded more than 200 songs with some of the best jazz musicians around, including "Strange Fruit" and "The Man I Love." Wearing her trademark gardenia in her hair, she continued giving memorable live performances until her death in 1959, when she was only 44.

DIGITALLY REMASTERED DIRECTLY FROM THE ORIGINAL ANALOG TAPES

CBS JAZZ MASTERPIECES

BESSIE SMITH
THE COLLECTION

LEFT: *Known as the Empress of the Blues, Bessie Smith never failed to put on a great show on the vaudeville stage.*

RIGHT: *The songs of Lady Day—Billie Holiday—resonated with the full range of her pain and her emotion.*

THE FIRST
VERVE
SESSIONS

**BILLIE
HOLIDAY**

*The 1952-54 recordings.
featuring Oscar Peterson.
Paul Quinichette,
Ray Brown, Charlie Shavers
Flip Phillips, Barney Kessel
and Freddie Green.*

Verve

A TWO
RECORD
SET

JAZZ

The great African-American pianist Jelly Roll Morton opened his newspaper in 1938 and read a claim in Ripley's *Believe It or Not* that W. C. Handy was the father of jazz. On the contrary, he wrote back, New Orleans was "the cradle of jazz and I, myself, happened to be the creator in 1902."

Maybe Morton invented jazz or maybe he did not—he was only 12 in 1902. However, he did invent a whole new way of playing the piano that, as he put it, "imitated a band." Morton had been brought up in the red-light district of Storyville in New Orleans. As a teenager, he worked as a house pianist in bars. While there, he was in the center of a musical phenomenon as a variety of different

BELOW: *Singing with her Georgia Jazz Band in 1925, Ma Rainey was one of the great jazz and blues vocalists.*

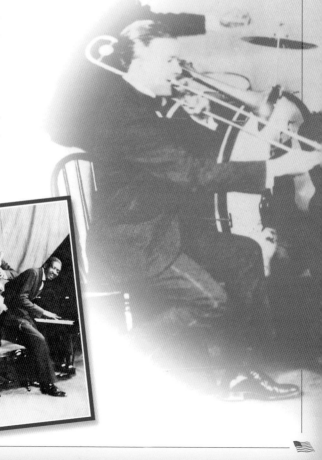

influences—Creole, Spanish, French, and, unmistakably, African-American—melded to create jazz.

Soon, New Orleans musicians were taking the new style north to Chicago. Joe "King" Oliver's Creole Jazz Band made the journey to Chicago's Southside. In 1923, another young man from New Orleans joined them there, destined to be one of the most famous jazz musicians of all time—Louis Armstrong.

LEFT: *Pianist Jelly Roll Morton, pictured here with his band, claimed to have created jazz in New Orleans.*

LOUIS ARMSTRONG

By the time Louis Armstrong joined the Creole Jazz Band, Oliver realized that the younger man had already overtaken him with the skill of his cornet playing. Armstrong learned to play music at the Jones Home for Colored Waifs, where he was sent when he was 11 for firing a gun in the air on New Year's Eve. He made the journey north with Oliver, then moved to New York, where he helped to make Harlem the entertainment hotbed of the 1920s and 1930s. One eyewitness describes Armstrong's unforgettable performance of "When You're Smiling." "Alternatively singing choruses and daubing with the handkerchief at throat, face, forehead (he perspires like a dying gladiator), while a diamond bracelet twinkles from his wrist."

> LOUIS ARMSTRONG
>
> *"What we play is life."*

LEFT: *Armstrong was a fantastic showman, whose soaring trumpet solos have never been forgotten.*
INSET: *Louis Armstrong, back row center, learned to play the horn in the band at the Jones Home for Colored Waifs in New Orleans.*

ABOVE RIGHT: *Swing dancing was all the rage in the Harlem nightclubs of the 1930s, and the fad soon swept the nation.*

SWING

Jazz was popular with both black and white listeners. Its bands were integrated, and so were some of the smaller clubs in which the best music was heard. This was a challenge to conservative whites. Bass player Milt Hinton described incidents in Fort Lauderdale, Florida, where he was playing in a black band in the 1930s. When white musicians they knew from Harlem's Cotton Club talked to them during the break, it enraged some of the

LEFT: *Duke Ellington's swing piano was the perfect accompaniment for Ella Fitzgerald's lyrical voice, made for singing scat.*

white audience. "Sometimes it would get so bad at intermission we couldn't get off the stand for a drink of water unless we had a police escort," he wrote. The big clubs, however, were still segregated. Although black musicians played at the Cotton Club, the audiences were white—and this segregation remained in place during the 1950s.

Yet throughout the 1920s and 1930s Harlem was hopping. Music and dance aficionados of all races loved it. The Apollo Theater, which would continue to draw audiences in the 1970s, hosted the biggest names in African-American entertainment every night. Among those singing there for the first time was Billie Holiday. "Some part

of it must have come across," she wrote later, describing the reaction to her rendition of "Trav'lin All Alone." "The whole joint quieted down. If someone dropped a pin, it would have sounded like a bomb. When I finished, everybody in the joint was crying in their beer, and I picked up 38 bucks up off the floor . . . I went out and bought a whole chicken and some baked beans."

Round the corner at the Cotton Club was Duke Ellington—also from New Orleans—moving on to swing hits like his 1932 "It Don't Mean a Thing if It Ain't Got That Swing." Swing, with its lively beat, was made for dancing, and it didn't get better than in Harlem's Savoy Ballroom. As Ellington played,

LEFT (INSET): *The Cotton Club was the most famous of Harlem's jazz nightspots, but the audiences were exclusively white.*

RIGHT: *Jazz did not recognize racial boundaries, and black and white musicians played together on recordings and in small, smoky clubs (where some of the best music was heard).*

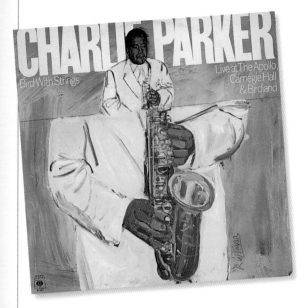

dancers matched every lick with a wilder move. Suddenly it was the era of the big swing bands. The Harlem sound spread across the country with recordings, radio, even Hollywood films. It lifted spirits through the Great Depression as couples everywhere did the lindy, "Harlem's newest dance craze."

The end of Prohibition in 1933 made jazz more respectable—illegal speakeasies had been the best places to hear good music—and African Americans continued to take it in new directions: Dizzy Gillespie brought Afro-Latin themes; Charlie Parker and Thelonius Monk found bebop; and Miles Davis fused jazz with cool, electric sounds. "Music is your own experience, your own thoughts, your wisdom," said Parker. "If you don't live it, it won't come out of your horn. They teach you there's a boundary line to music. But, man, there's no boundary line to art."

It was the era of bebop, a revolt against the big bands and their commercial exploiters. "Bop comes out of them dark days," says a character in a novel by African-American writer Langston Hughes. "That's why real Bop is mad, wild, frantic, crazy—and not to be dug unless you've seen dark days, too. Folks who ain't suffered much cannot play Bop, neither appreciate it." The bebop players created an individualist sound of swirling solo improvisations made by jamming together in a musicians' hangout called Minton's.

TOP LEFT: *Saxophonist Charlie Parker pioneered the swirling sound of bebop in the 1940s.*

LEFT: *Hugely influential since the late 1940s, Miles Davis brought about a new style of "cool" jazz.*

THE BIG VOICE

The pioneering all-black Broadway show *Shuffle Along* (1921), featuring the hit song "I'm Just Wild About Harry," included an unknown chorus girl called Josephine Baker and an assistant piano player, Nat Cole (later King). Baker would become the toast of Paris with her banana skirt and leopard on a leash. Among the show's cast was a former law student and athlete named Paul Robeson.

At the same time, Marian Anderson, an African American from Philadelphia, was singing in her church choir—nearly 20 years before prejudice put her name on the front page of the world's newspapers. In 1939, the Daughters of the American Revolution refused to let her sing at Constitution Hall in Washington, D.C. because she was black. The decision was greeted with outrage. Eleanor Roosevelt resigned from the Daughters and arranged for Anderson to sing at the Lincoln Memorial at Easter. The performance was seen by over 75,000 people.

Robeson's deep bass voice became one of the most recognized voices in the world. Although he trained as a lawyer, he could not keep off the stage. He was also a tireless civil rights activist, as well as a Communist.

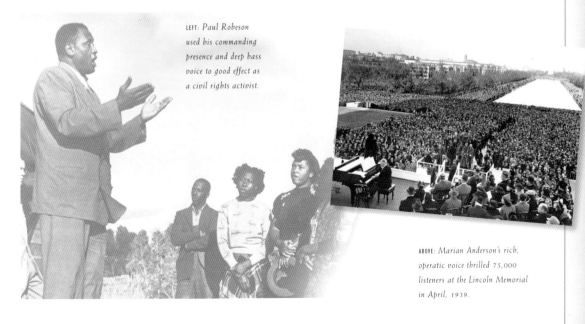

LEFT: *Paul Robeson used his commanding presence and deep bass voice to good effect as a civil rights activist.*

ABOVE: *Marian Anderson's rich, operatic voice thrilled 75,000 listeners at the Lincoln Memorial in April, 1939.*

ROCK AND ROLL

The writer Maya Angelou grew up in San Francisco in the 1940s and 1950s. She described herself listening to vocalists like Billie Holiday and Nat King Cole midmorning, bebop giants like Parker and Gillespie after lunch, and blues in the late afternoon.

In the 1940s and 1950s, black rhythm and blues combos, slimmed down versions of the big swing bands, were making the music of the moment. Showmanship and style fronted musical virtuosity. Entertainers such as Fats Domino, Louis Jordan, and Dinah Washington attracted fans both white and black. A white DJ, Allen Freed, heard the black rhythm and blues sound and named it "rock and roll." By renaming it, a white audience claimed it, and the rhythm and blues sound became a national phenomenon.

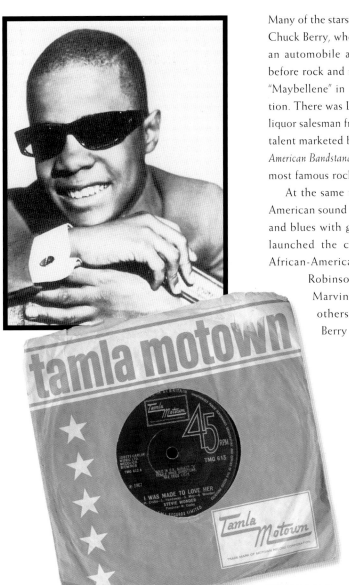

Many of the stars were African-American. There was Chuck Berry, who grew up in St. Louis and became an automobile assembler and then a hairdresser before rock and roll. Sure enough, his first hit was "Maybellene" in 1955, the name of a hair preparation. There was Little Richard, the son of a bootleg liquor salesman from Georgia. Chubby Checker, his talent marketed by white impresario Dick Clark on *American Bandstand*, invented the twist, probably the most famous rock and roll dance of all.

At the same time, another distinctive African-American sound was emerging, combining rhythm and blues with gospel. The record label Motown launched the careers of some of the greatest African-American soul artists, such as Smokey Robinson, Diana Ross, Stevie Wonder, Marvin Gaye, Gladys Knight and others. Motown was the brainchild of Berry Gordy Jr., who was writing songs

FAR LEFT: *Chuck Berry's creative songwriting and rapid-fire guitar combined for a distinctive and very popular R&B sound.*

LEFT (INSET): *Little Richard brought the emotional power of Gospel music to his sax-led rock 'n' roll sound.*

ABOVE (INSET) AND LEFT: *Stevie Wonder started recording with Motown when he was only 12 years old and went on to international renown.*

RIGHT: *Since her beginning with the Supremes, Diana Ross has catapulted to international stardom.*

ABOVE: *Along with his group the Miracles, Smokey Robinson had numerous Soul hits in the 1960s.*

and managing rhythm and blues groups in Detroit, Michigan. With his colleagues, he created the Motown sound, offering luxurious harmonies and lyrics that were clean enough for radio and TV. This time a black impresario was going to make sure that African Americans were making the profit from their creativity. By 1971, hits like "Baby Love" and "I Heard It Through the Grapevine" had made Motown the most profitable black-owned company in the United States.

RAP AND HIP-HOP

Rap is the latest in a long line of African-American sounds to attract audiences around the world. It emerged in the 1970s in the clubs of the Bronx, in New York City, where mobile DJs competed with each other, innovating the ways they spun records and presented songs. As the DJs mixed a soundtrack, MCs rapped to the beat, speaking with rhythm and rhyme. The hip-hop aesthetic is African-American to the core. It takes influences from rhythm and blues artists like James Brown, from street jive talk, African music, and folk traditions like playing the dozens—exaggerating exaggerations—or signifying—topping each other's insults. From its street beginnings, rap music has become a global, commercial phenomenon. The hip-hop style has had a major influence on everything from fashion to language. Rap had its first hit record in 1979 with "Rapper's Delight" by the Sugar Hill Gang. However, it is also a living art, still created in the neighborhoods where it originated.

RIGHT: *"Rapper's Delight",*
from the Sugar Hill Gang out of
Brooklyn, reached #36 on
Billboard's Top 40, making it
the first crossover rap hit.

AFRICAN-AMERICAN IMAGES

> "He looked in vain into the stalls for the butcher who had sold fresh meat twice a week, on market days," wrote the African-American Ohio writer Charles Chesnutt, describing the experience of going back home to the Old South. "He felt a genuine thrill of pleasure when he recognized the red bandana turban of old Aunt Lyddy, the ancient Negro woman who had sold him gingerbread and fried fish, and told him weird tales of witchcraft and conjuration."

The passage comes from Chesnutt's 1900 novel *House Behind the Cedars*. He specialized in retelling these African-American tales of superstition. He wove together two continents. This combination—folk mysticism mixed with verve and sophistication—is in so much of African-American art and culture. It is found in the energy of paintings like Archibald Motley's *Chicken Shack* and in the poems and books of Countee Cullen, Zora Neale Hurston, or Toni Morrison.

RIGHT: *Toni Morrison, the first African-American winner of the Nobel Prize for Literature.*

BELOW: *Ntozake Shange (right) performs a scene in her play* For Colored Girls Who Have Considered Suicide When the Rainbow is Enuf, *a national hit in 1977.*

RIGHT: *Zora Neale Hurston, short-story writer and novelist. Her writing detailed many aspects of African-American life in the South.*

89

ABOVE: *The poet Langston Hughes was one of the leading writers of the Harlem Renaissance.*

RIGHT: *During the 1920s, Harlem's nightclubs were hotbeds of jazz and dance innovation.*

THE HARLEM RENAISSANCE AND AFRICAN-AMERICAN WRITING

There had been black writers before the Harlem Renaissance of the 1920s. In 1773, Phillis Wheatley, a young African-born slave in Boston, Massachusetts, published her first volume of poetry—but not before she had to present herself in front of a group of 18 of Boston's most venerable white men to prove that she really was the author. They found it inconceivable that an African woman could be capable of such artistry.

Until the Civil War put an end to slavery, many African-American writers were concerned with campaigning against social injustice. They published pamphlets, books, and memoirs, such as slave narratives (*see page 26*), to sway people to the abolitionist cause, and creative writing had a lower profile.

From the end of the nineteenth century, however, African-American fiction shone. For instance, Frances Harper's *Iola Leroy* was one of the first in a series of seminal works by African-American women, and Charles W. Chesnutt created memorable fiction.

During World War I, African-American singers, students, writers, musicians, and revolutionaries began to congregate in Harlem, creating a vibrant moment of cultural history. "It was the period when the Negro was in vogue," wrote Langston Hughes.

From the 1920s, jazz innovation was surprising even the musicians themselves. New York's white avant-garde began to throng Harlem in search of new sounds, new dances, and new experiences. In the Cotton Club, the finest black musicians played for exclusively white audiences. It was a different atmosphere than in the South. While growing up in Mississippi, the novelist Richard Wright told Gertrude Stein that he had been forbidden to play swing records, blues, or jazz. However, when he went north to Chicago, "White boys would corner me and tell me the deep meanings buried in a solo trumpet." Harlem made that possible.

It was on the literary front that the Harlem Renaissance marked the biggest change in national sentiment. White publishing houses now began to offer widespread distribution of the works of African-American writers. This altered the outlook for black writers permanently. However, real creative fire burned from the mid-1920s to the mid-1930s. Those years produced the poetry of Langston Hughes and Claude McKay, innovative novels such as Jean Toomer's *Cane* and Jessie Fauset's *There Is Confusion*, and short stories by Zora Neale Hurston, whose acclaimed novel, *Their Eyes Were Watching God*, was not published until 1937.

RIGHT: *Phillis Wheatley, born in Africa and sold into slavery in the United States, was the first African American to publish a book, in 1773.*

LEFT: *The glamour of 1920s Harlem fueled wider interest in African-American arts.*

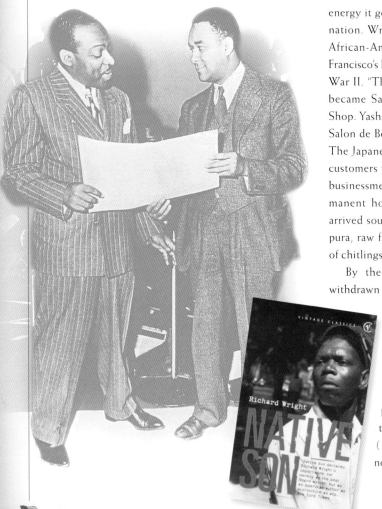

THE BLACK ARTS MOVEMENT

Although the Harlem Renaissance was brought short by the Great Depression, the cultural energy it generated continued to spread across the nation. Writer Maya Angelou described how the African-American influence took hold of San Francisco's Fillmore district at the outbreak of World War II. "The Yakamoto Sea Food Market quietly became Sammy's Shoe Shine Parlor and Smoke Shop. Yashigira's Hardware metamorphosed into La Salon de Beauté owned by Miss Clorinda Jackson. The Japanese shops which sold products to Nisei customers were taken over by enterprising Negro businessmen, and in less than a year became permanent homes away from home for the newly arrived southern blacks. Where the odors of tempura, raw fish, and cha had dominated, the aroma of chitlings, greens, and ham hocks now prevailed."

By the 1950s, jazz moved from cool and withdrawn to angry and demanding. A second wave of African-American writing was emerging: the social realism of Richard Wright's *Native Son* (1940), Ralph Ellison's *The Invisible Man* (1952), Ann Petry's *The Street* (1946), James Baldwin's *Go Tell It On The Mountain* (1953), and the poems of Gwendolyn Brooks, who won the 1950 Pulitzer Prize for "Annie Allen" (1949) ("It is brave to be involved/To be not fearful to be unresolved").

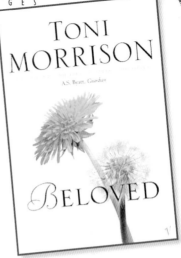

Inspired by the radical movements of the 1960s, the Black Arts Movement consciously moved away from what it termed a "white aesthetic" and looked for inspiration to the African-American community as well as Africa: Amin Baraka and Larry Neale defined the movement in their anthology, *Black Fire* (1968). Poetry flourished, with works by Sonia Sanchez, Nikki Giovanni, Ishmael Reed, and others.

By the early 1980s, a generation of African-American women writers had emerged. Plays like Ntozake Shange's *For Colored Girls Who Have Considered Suicide When the Rainbow Is Enuf* stunned audiences across the United States in 1977. Toni Morrison became the first African American to win the Nobel Prize for Literature, with *Beloved* (1987), based on the true story of a runaway slave. In 1993, Maya Angelou was the first African-American writer to read a poem at a presidential inauguration.

It was a flowering of talent based on a new kind of freedom. "We younger Negro artists who create now intend to express our individual dark skinned selves without fear or shame," Langston Hughes had written several decades earlier. "If white people are pleased, we are glad. If they are not, it doesn't matter. We know we are beautiful. And ugly, too. If colored people are pleased we are glad. If they are not, their displeasure doesn't matter. We build our temple for tomorrow, strong as we know how, and we stand on top of the mountain, free within ourselves."

BELOW: *Poet Maya Angelou reading a poem at the inauguration of President Bill Clinton in 1993.*

ABOVE: *Toni Morrison won the Nobel Prize for* Beloved *(1987), based on the true story of a runaway slave.*

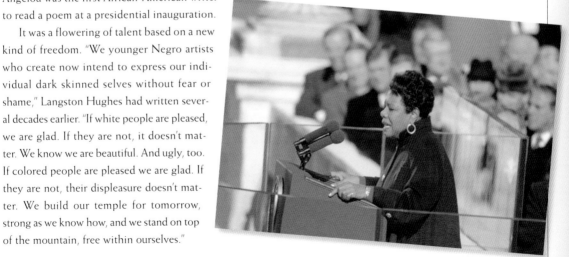

BELOW: *Chicago DJ Al Benson chartered a plane to drop 5,000 copies of the U.S. Constitution over his native Mississippi in a bid to encourage political awareness in the state. In the 1950s and 1960s, many African-American DJs were committed to the civil rights movement.*

RIGHT: *Student Rufus P. Turner became the first African American to operate a radio station when he was chosen to operate the facility at the St. Augustine Roman Catholic Church in Washington, D.C.*

94

AFRICAN-AMERICAN RADIO

Radio was the critical medium in the first half of the twentieth century. Although advertisers and sponsors tried to exclude African Americans for fear of alienating southern listeners, stations around the country were soon broadcasting Duke Ellington and Paul Robeson to new audiences.

In 1929, African Americans first put their own stamp on the medium with Jack Cooper's popular program *The All-Negro Hour*. Cooper helped to pioneer the disc jockey format and was the first to target news and sports coverage to black audiences. His colleague Al Benson, who came to Chicago from Mississippi in the 1930s, brought street culture to the airwaves and was much copied by black and white producers alike.

WDIA in Memphis, Tennessee, became the first U.S. radio station to have an all-black broadcasting staff. It featured musicians like B. B. King and Rufus Thomas, playing rhythm and blues, swing, and gospel, and won the nickname "The Goodwill Station" for its work with the African-American community. Soon enough, listeners throughout the country were enjoying pioneering African-American broadcasters like Jocko Henderson in New York, Dr. Hepcat in Austin, Texas, and Martha Jean "The Queen" Steinberg.

By the 1950s and 1960s, black DJs and broadcasters like Gatemouth Moore, Jockey Jack Gibson, and Roy Wood were the first messengers of the emerging civil rights movement. They interviewed the leaders, advising and calming during the most dangerous moments.

RIGHT: *Country-blues singer Rufus Thomas, working as a DJ for WDIA in Memphis in 1973. WDIA was the first station in the country to have an all-black staff.*

LEFT AND ABOVE: *D. W. Griffiths'*
film, The Birth of a Nation
(1915), was a racist retelling
of the story of the Civil War
and Reconstruction, starting
from the first transportation
of slaves to America. It was
undoubtedly powerful cinema,
but its evident bias incensed
African Americans. In later
years, the NAACP picketed
cinemas showing the movie,
calling for a ban on hate movies.

RENAISSANCE HOLLYWOOD

The damage that could be caused by Hollywood racial stereotyping became only too clear with the 1915 release of *Birth of a Nation*, with its elegiac tribute to the lynch mobs. "It's like writing history with lightning," said President Woodrow Wilson after a private showing.

As the movie industry settled down in California, there was not much to balance this impression of African Americans. A grizzled bum appeared in *Beggars of Life* (1928), and a seaman was played by the boxer George Godfrey in *Old Ironsides* (1926). There were black parts in *Showboat* (1927), *Uncle Tom's Cabin* (1927), and of course *St. Louis Blues* (1929). However, most African Americans taking refuge in the movies saw themselves portrayed as servants, convicts, or maybe racehorse or boxing trainers.

Birth of a Nation had one positive effect, though. It inspired the African-American moviemaker Oscar Micheaux to begin work. Micheaux had been a Pullman porter, homesteader, and novelist selling his books door to door. He was also a legendary entrepreneur. Until recently, the only surviving copies of his early work were of the 1924 *Body and Soul*. Recently, his earlier movies *Within Our Gates* and *The Symbol of the Unconquered* have come to light and enthused a new generation. After overcoming bankruptcy, Micheaux returned to remake his autobiography as *The Exile* (1931), later breaking into talkies with The *Girl from Chicago* (1932) and

Swing (1938). Unfortunately, two decades or so passed before mainstream Hollywood began to portray African Americans in anything other than stereotyped cameo parts. Not until Sidney Poitier came on the scene did Hollywood come up with a major African-American star.

BELOW: *Paul Robeson in Showboat (1936). There were few good role models for African Americans in the movies at that time—many parts were simply racial stereotypes.*

RIGHT: *Although he was criticized for not being radical, Sidney Poitier chose to work in movies that confronted themes of racism and race relations.*

DIFFERENT BY FAITH, SKIN AND CALLING BUT WHAT A WONDERFUL ADVENTURE THEY SHARED!

"He is not of our faith nor of our skin," said Mother Maria. "But he is a man of greatness."

SIDNEY POITIER

RALPH NELSON'S

Lilies of the Field

LILIA SKALA · STANLEY ADAMS

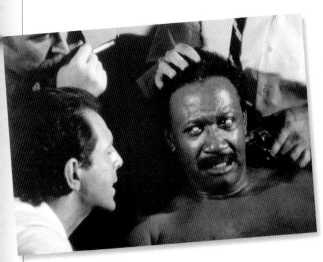

LEFT (INSET):*With* Lilies of the Field, *Sidney Poitier became the first black man to win an Oscar for Best Actor.*

ABOVE: *Melvin Van Peebles in* Sweet Sweetback's Baadasssss Song, *the movie that inspired the "blaxploitation" genre.*

SIDNEY POITIER AND AFTER

Born in Miami, Florida, Poitier emigrated to Jamaica as a child. At 16, he returned to the United States and began working for the American Negro Theater as a janitor in exchange for acting lessons. He built his reputation standing in for Harry Belafonte for one night in the play *Days of our Youth* on Broadway. Hollywood called in 1950. Poitier's movie work eventually led to an Oscar for his performance in *Lilies of the Field* in 1963. (That same year, he returned to the stage in the first Broadway play by an African-American playwright, Lorraine Hansberry's *A Raisin in the Sun*, the story of a black family confronting the problems of segregation.) Poitier was criticized for the unreal perfection of the characters he portrayed, who seemed to fit in better with a liberal white view of how black people should be rather than with African-American realities.

Not until the late 1960s, reflecting progress made by the civil rights movement, did Hollywood dare to present more streetwise, edgier visions of African-American life. Black moviemaker Melvin Van Peebles inspired a whole genre with his movie *Sweet Sweetback's Baadasssss Song* about an escaped prisoner who is helped by his numerous lovers in a Los Angeles ghetto. Following the rejection of this movie by the Hollywood studios, Van Peebles financed it himself. As Van Peebles tells it, he looked in the mirror one morning after the final rejection came and said, "I think I am a studio, therefore I am a studio." Hollywood soon followed Van Peebles's lead, offering up "blaxploitation" movies such as *Shaft* (1971) and *Superfly* (1972). Both featured urban black heroes or comedic reflections of contemporary African-American cultural life and style, like Michael Shultz's 1976 movie *Car Wash*.

The mainstreaming of African-American images in the 1970s encouraged a new generation of movie-makers, such as Spike Lee, who wanted to make movies on their own terms, representing black culture fairly and free of stereotypes. "I've never really thought of myself as a spokesperson for 35 million African Americans," Lee says. "All my views have been solely my views, and I think that there are African-American people who agree with me, but we also have African Americans who don't agree . . . It is a fallacy that all of my critics are white."

Lee burst into Hollywood with *She's Gotta Have It* in 1986, marking a turning point for African-American movies. "That was also the year the black folk suffered through Prince in *Under the Cherry Moon*, Eddie Murphy in *Golden Child*, Whoopi Goldberg in *Jumpin' Jack Flash*, and Rae Dawn Chong in *Soul Man*," said New York's *Village Voice* ten years later. Then *She's Gotta Have It* opened in New York City, and as Nelson George notes in *Blackface*: 'The world of black film changes forever.' " Lee's uncompromising movies attracted both black and white audiences. *Do the Right Thing* (1989), about tensions between communities in New York City, was commercially successful and challenged preconceptions about race relations.

That African Americans have firmly taken their place in Hollywood was confirmed by the 2001 Academy Awards, when black stars triumphed, with Denzel Washington winning for best actor and Halle Berry for best actress.

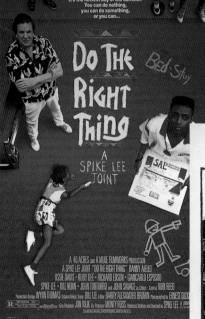

LEFT: *Spike Lee made his big-screen directorial debut with* She's Gotta Have It (1986), *an often gentle, comic movie about black New Yorkers. With* Do the Right Thing (1989), *he took a direct and sometimes shocking look at race tensions in New York's Bed-Stuy neighborhood.*

ABOVE: *Based on Alice Walker's bestselling novel of the same name,* The Color Purple *is the story of Celie, a southern black woman, and her political and social awakening. It was a huge commercial success.*

TELEVISION

The portrayal of African Americans on television followed the same broad pattern as in the movies. Although African-American performers were featured on television from its launch in 1948, they generally fit the stereotypical roles: "mammies" or comic performers who acted out black caricatures in the vaudeville tradition.

Not until the late 1960s was comedian Bill Cosby able break the race barrier on the small screen when he was cast as a secret agent in *I Spy*, a role for which he won his first Emmy. Cosby, one of America's most popular entertainers, went on to break new ground with subsequent projects, too. His animated children's series, *Fat Albert and the Cosby Kids*, portrayed young lives in the slums of Philadelphia with humor, teaching positive lessons along the way. Additionally, *The Cosby Show*, which debuted in 1984, was a positive vision of African-American family life (albeit an upper-middle-class one).

Throughout the 1970s and 1980s, mini-series presented the most captivating and balanced images of African Americans. They started with *The Autobiography of Miss Jane Pittman* (1974) and continued to *The Women of Brewster Place* (1988), produced by Oprah Winfrey. *Roots* (1977), written by Alex Haley, the ghostwriter for Malcolm X's (see page 66) influential posthumous autobiography, really broke the mold. Bringing home the realities

JAMES BALDWIN

"We, in the ghetto then, knew very little about Paul Robeson. We knew very little about anything black, in fact, and this was not our fault. Those of us who found out more than the schools were willing to teach us did so at the price of becoming unmanageable, isolated, and, indeed, subversive. The south was simply the hell which our parents had survived, and fled. Harlem was our rat and roach infested haven."

BELOW: *Bill Cosby (shown here with costar Robert Culp) broke Hollywood color lines when he was cast as a secret agent in* I Spy *in 1966. He went on to create some of TV's most popular sitcoms and children's series.*

of racism throughout American history to a receptive audience, it attracted the highest ratings of any TV series in American history.

The cast of *Roots* included the young African-American actress Oprah Winfrey, who went on to prove that African Americans can wield real power in television. The Mississippi-born Winfrey rose through the news and talk show route, eventually beating Phil Donahue at his own game and becoming the most popular syndicated talk show host in television history. Her "Oprah's Bookclub" segments promoted the work of many African-American novelists, as well as that of white writers. Her endorsement could make a book a bestseller in an instant. With her production company Harpo, Winfrey is credited with making some high-quality programming, including made-for-TV movies based on notable African-American fiction.

Oprah Winfrey is not the only African American to have taken control behind the cameras. Growing black influence in TV production has led to a number of other TV shows with African-American themes, such as Quincy Jones's *The Fresh Prince of Bel Air*, and Keenan Ivory's Wayans's irreverent program *In Living Color.*

ABOVE: *Oprah Winfrey is one of the most powerful and influential
people in the American media today.*

AFRICAN AMERICANS AND SPORT

Mohammad Ali was a great boxer, proud to be African-American, bold, revolutionary, and inspirational. It is hard to imagine professional sports in the United States today without African Americans. Yet, until the mid-twentieth century, that was exactly the situation. The progress toward full integration was fraught with complications, courage, and persistance. Take Bill Pickett, the African-American rodeo star and inventor of the art of bulldogging. Look at Marshall W. "Major" Taylor, who beat every leading cyclist in the world at the end of the nineteenth century, learning to deal with the dirty tricks used by those determined to keep sports segregated. Learn about the women's basketball squad sponsored by the *Philadelphia Tribune* in 1930, the first African-American female team to make a major impact in the United States. Look at Joseph Rice, who successfully took Miami Springs to the Supreme Court because African-American golfers were restricted to one day a week on the city's only golf course. His fight paved the way for people of color, like Tiger Woods, five decades later.

> *"I don't believe all this stuff I say,"* Mohammad Ali told spectators just before his famous Rumble in the Jungle to regain his world heavyweight boxing title in 1974. *"I say it only to make people angry—then I go to the bank laughin'."* Mohammad Ali was the real thing.

BOXING

Boxing was one sport in which African Americans were long allowed to participate. Banned from taking part in nearly all sports, slaves were sometimes allowed to box—as long as it was only against each other. A free black from Staten Island, New York, William Richmond, became the first African American to contend for a world title in any sport. That was in 1805. He also trained the next black champion, Tom Molineaux, a former slave who earned his freedom by winning a boxing bout.

Nearly a century on, George "Little Chocolate" Dixon beat the British featherweight champion Nunc Wallace to become world champion in 1890. Dixon went on to beat the white amateur Jack Skelly in New Orleans two years later. However, the authorities were so horrified by his victory that they managed to prevent mixed-race bouts for a generation.

Texas-born Jack Johnson changed all that. After Johnson won the heavyweight championship in San Francisco, knocking down reigning champion Jim Jeffries twice, 13 African Americans were murdered around the United States in racially motivated incidents. Not until the emergence of Joe Louis, the so-called Brown Bomber, two decades later was an African-American boxer able to break through into the mainstream.

TOP LEFT: *Bill Pickett was a star of the American rodeo circuit and was credited with inventing "bulldogging."*

LEFT: *Tiger Woods became the first golfer to hold all four major titles at the same time. His phenomenal skill has allowed him to dominate his sport.*

RIGHT: *Charismatic and entertaining, Jack Johnson became the first African-American heavyweight champion in 1908. The white boxing establishment struggled to find a "great white hope" who could beat him.*

JAMES E. PEPPER WHISKY
"BORN WITH THE REPUBLIC."

WORLD'S CHAMPIONSHIP BATTLE JULY 4 1910

JOE LOUIS

Joe Louis Barrow was a product of the Great Migration. Born in 1914 in Chambers County, Alabama, he moved to Detroit as a child. When he was 17, Joe's mother gave him 50 cents for violin lessons. Instead, he spent the money on renting a locker at the Brewster East Side Gymnasium and began training to be a boxer.

When Louis knocked out Primo Carnera in 1935, he became a hero in the African-American

BELOW: *In his 71 professional bouts, Joe Louis—the Brown Bomber—was only defeated three times.*

community. "When I walked in the church, you'd have thought it was the second coming of Christ," he wrote later. He described how the minister "talked about how God gave people certain gifts . . . and through my fighting I was to uplift the spirit of my race. I must make the whole world know that Negro people were strong, fair, and decent. He said I was one of the chosen. I thought to myself: 'Jesus Christ, am I all that?' "

Louis became a national hero when he won the world heavyweight championships in 1937. "When we heard that Louis had knocked out [James J.] Braddock in the eighth round, we went crazy," remembered history teacher Timuel Black from Chicago. "I remember the band was playing a really smooth 'Moonglow,' and that my heart glowed as well when they announced Louis the champ . . . The mostly white crowd at Comiskey Park was crying, shouting, laughing. Horns were tooting. They were singing in the streets. After the fight, Louis and his entourage walked over to the Armory at 35th and Giles for the fun. It was bedlam outside and inside."

When Louis was knocked out by the German Max Schmeling in 1936, the Nazi press celebrated that the black race had been checked—and rioting began in Harlem. However, the entire United States was to celebrate two years later when Louis knocked Schmeling out in the rematch, seeing it as a victory against the Nazi regime. Joe Louis held the world heavyweight championship for 11 years and eight months.

RIGHT: *Joe Louis holds up the fist that won him the heavyweight crown over James Braddock in Chicago in 1937. He defended that title a record 25 times, achieving knockouts in 21 of those matches.*

BELOW: *This souvenir issue of* The Ring *commemorates Louis's bout against German boxer Max Schmeling. Louis's victory in their 1938 rematch led to national rejoicing, especially in Harlem and other black neighborhoods across the country.*

FAR RIGHT: *Cassius Clay (as Mohammad Ali, pictured right, was then known) talks to the press after receiving a Grand Jury indictment for his refusal to be inducted into the armed forces. He was later imprisoned for draft evasion.*

BELOW: *A vociferous advocate of African-American rights, Mohammad Ali was proud of his heritage and continues to be an inspiration to young African-American sportsmen to this day.*

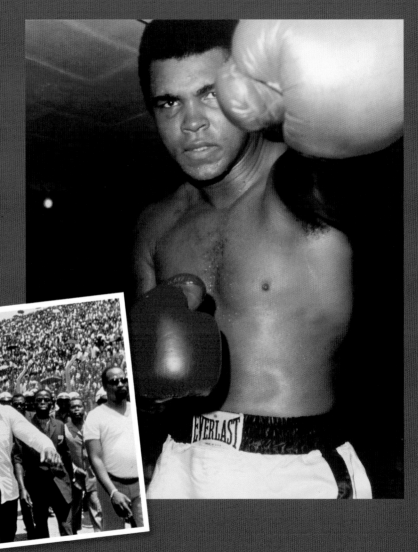

MOHAMMAD ALI

There were many great African-American fighters like Sugar Ray Robinson, Floyd Patterson, and Sonny Liston. However, none was like Mohammad Ali, born Cassius Marcellus Clay in 1942 in Louisville, Kentucky.

Apart from his skill in the ring, the young Clay was bold and proud. "For God's sake, after you beat a white opponent, don't smile," Joe Louis was constantly advised. Ali did not accept that. Jack Johnson, the first African-American heavyweight champion, might have introduced boasting and taunting opponents, but Ali made it into an art.

Clay began boxing when he was 12, winning a gold medal in the 1960 Rome Olympics. He was disappointed that racial prejudice meant that he was not welcomed back as an American hero in his segregated hometown, and lost his medal after throwing it into a bayou following a chase by white racists attempting to steal it.

The day after Clay beat Sonny Liston for the world title the second time, in 1965, he announced his conversion to Islam and joined the Nation of Islam (*see page 67*), changing his name to Mohammad Ali. He also became an outspoken opponent of the Vietnam War, was imprisoned for 29 months for draft evasion, and was stripped of his title. He explained it in one of his rhymes:

Keep asking me, no matter how long,
On the war in Viet Nam, I sing this song:
I ain't got no quarrel with them Viet Cong.

Ali won back the world title in an extraordinary fight with George Foreman in Kinshasa in the Congo (then called Zaire)—the Rumble in the Jungle. "I'm the only black man in the world standin' up for my people," said Ali at the time. "All the rednecks and Uncle Toms are pullin' for me to lose. I'm gonna whip George Foreman, not for money, not so I can have a blonde on both arms— so I can go with blacks, use it to practice what Elijah teaches." Ali finally retired from the ring in 1980—the only person to have regained his title a record three times.

JESSE OWENS

While Joe Louis undermined Nazi race propaganda, in one magnificent week in August 1936, Jesse Owens left Adolf Hitler's racial philosophy in tatters. While competing in the Berlin Olympics, with Hitler himself watching, Owens won no fewer than four gold medals, for the 100-meter dash, the long jump, the 200-meter dash, and the 400-meter relay, shattering the Olympic record on each occasion.

Another child of the Great Migration, Owens was born in Alabama but moved to an impoverished Cleveland, Ohio, when he was eight. He discovered his flair for running when he was a boy.

Owens was endlessly hard up. Hitler's fury that an African American had starred in the Games brought Owens worldwide fame. However, he was unable to get a job even after his triumphant return from Berlin. "When I came back to my native country, after all the stories about Hitler, I couldn't ride in the front of the bus," he said later. "I had to go to the back door. I couldn't live where I wanted. I wasn't invited to shake hands with Hitler, but I wasn't invited to the White House to shake hands with the President either." Nearly 40 years passed before President Gerald Ford awarded Owens the Presidential Medal of Freedom, the nation's highest civilian award.

LEFT: *Jesse Owens was extremely talented, setting records as a high-school and college athlete even before his legendary achievements at the 1936 Berlin Olympics. However, after his return from Berlin, unlike other athletes, sponsorships did not come his way, and he was forced to drop out of college to support his family.*

ABOVE: *The American relay team that won gold in the 400-meter relay race at the Berlin Olympics in 1936, from left to right: Jesse Owens, Ralph Metcalfe, Foy Draper, and Frank Wykoff. In addition to the gold medal, the team also broke the Olympic record.*

RIGHT: *Headlines report that Hitler refused to shake hands with African-American athletes Jesse Owens and Cornelius Johnson, who were competing in the 1936 Olympic Games in Berlin.*

BASEBALL

In the 1880s—as African Americans were coming to terms with freedom—two brothers, Welday and Moses Walker, became the first black men to play professional baseball in teams belonging to the National Association of Baseball (the precursor to today's Major League). They were also the last to do so for many years once a gentlemen's agreement barred African Americans from the big leagues.

All-black professional teams were formed instead—the first was the Cuban Giants in Long Island, New York. The teams played each other around the country, organizing their own league system in the 1920s with the Negro National League and the Negro Eastern League. These teams played great baseball and launched the careers of Josh Gibson (the so-called Black Babe Ruth because he hit 89 home runs in one season), Judy Johnson of the Pittsburgh Crawfords, and Satchel Paige of the Chattanooga Black Lookouts and the New Orleans Black Pelicans.

Some Major League managers tried to hire African Americans by calling the players Hispanic or Native American. In 1901, John McGraw, manager of the Baltimore Orioles, tried to get black second baseman Charlie Grant into the game by calling him Charlie Tokohama and passing him off as a Cherokee. However, they were swimming against the tide of the baseball establishment.

JACKIE ROBINSON

When he stepped onto Ebbets Field on April 15, 1947, for the Brooklyn Dodgers, Jackie Robinson became the first African American in the twentieth century to play baseball in the major leagues. The Dodgers' trainer, Branch Rickey, had been quietly plotting to bring African-American players to the team. "I had to get the right man off the field," said Rickey later. "I couldn't come with a man to break down a tradition, which had in it centered and concentrated all the prejudices of a great many people north and south, unless he was good. He must justify himself upon the positive principle of merit . . . But more dangerous to me, at that time, and even now, is the wrong man off the field . . . I wanted a man of exceptional intelligence, a man who was able to grasp and control the responsibilities of himself to his race and could carry that load."

Robinson was intelligent, and was not prepared just to take insults. As an officer in the war, he had faced a court martial at Fort Hood, Texas, for refusing to obey an order to move to the back of a bus. Because this was ruled a violation of Army regulations, he was exonerated. On tour with the Dodgers, he would not hesitate to protest against hotels that refused to let him stay with his team, or against teams that refused to hire African-American players.

LEFT: *Jackie Robinson was the first African American to play major league baseball, integrating the game for good.*

BASKETBALL

African-American teams shone throughout the early history of basketball. Many of their players were national figures. The Harlem Globetrotters, for example, were the top black club team, and they were admired the length and breadth of the country for their dexterous ball handling and shooting skills. Black and white club teams could play each other—but the teams themselves were always segregated.

When the Basketball Association of America became the National Basketball Association before the 1949–50 season, no African Americans were listed on any of the league's rosters. That year, Earl Lloyd was the first to play in an NBA game, and, in 1951, the Boston Celtics signed Chuck Cooper. Once in the NBA, African-American players were quick to distinguish themselves: William Fenton Russell in the 1950s, Lew Alcindor—who changed his name to Kareem Abdul-Jabbar—in the 1960s, Dr. J in the 1970s, "Magic" Johnson in the 1980s, and Michael Jordan in the 1990s.

By the time the NBA integrated, all-black teams had to find ways to adapt. The Harlem Globetrotters responded to the end of segregation by creating exhibition games around their tricks, fancy passes, and extraordinary dribbling skills. By the 1950s, there was so much demand for the Globetrotters that two parallel teams toured

LEFT: *Chuck Cooper of the Boston Celtics (right) and Nat Clifton of the New York Knicks fight for the ball. Cooper was one of the first African Americans to sign with an NBA team.*

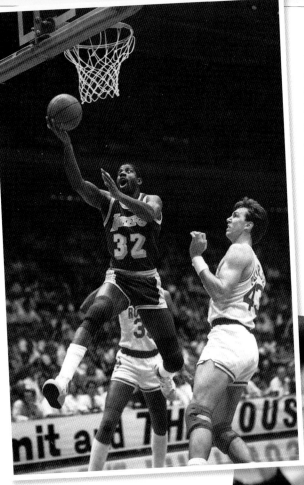

the east and west of the United States at the same time. They also played many international dates. Globetrotters Meadowlark Lemon and Fred "Curly" Neal became famous around the world. Additionally, future NBA champion Wilt Chamberlain launched his professional basketball career by playing a year with the Globetrotters.

BELOW: *During the 1990s, Michael Jordan played outstanding basketball for the Chicago Bulls. He was also a member of the Dream Team, the U.S.A.'s entry in the 1992 Olympic Games in Barcelona.*

ABOVE: *"Magic" Johnson, one of the stars of the 1980s, drives in for a lay-up, scoring for the Los Angeles Lakers.*

THE FUTURE

CELEBRATIONS

Today African Americans are adding their own celebrations to the national calendar. By creating their own rituals, they are affirming a sense of community and identity. By achieving recogni- tion of these rituals throughout the United States, they are continuing to contribute to the rich tapestry of American culture.

Juneteenth, commemorating the end of slavery in the United States, is one example. Events throughout the country on and around June 19

each year celebrate freedom, and also focus on education and self-improvement. Taking place on the Mall in Washington, D.C., in large cities and small towns, and in schools and homes, performances, lectures, exhibits, and parties celebrate African-American achievement, remember the past, and look to the future. Juneteenth is recognized as a state holiday in Texas and Delaware. Numerous groups at both the state and national level campaign for further recognition.

Kwanzaa

Kwanzaa is another holiday that unites African-American communities. With its roots in ancient African culture but its reality in the present day, it was created in 1966 by Maulana Karenga, an academic and activist. Kwanzaa takes place between December 26 and January 1 each year. Each day is devoted to one of seven principles: *umoja* (unity), *kujichagulia* (self-determination), *ujima* (collective responsibility), *ujamaa* (cooperative economics), *nia* (purpose), *kuumba* (creativity), and *imani* (faith). In the evening, families gather to light one of seven candles (one black, three red, and three green—the colors of Kwanzaa) in a Kinara, a special candleholder, and to share a meal. On December 31, a Karumu—the Kwanzaa feast—is held, bringing communities together for a communal supper. The holiday ends on January 1, with the Siku ya Taamuli, a day of meditation for self-assessment and reaffirmation.

LEFT: *"Juneteenth" (June 19) commemorates both the end of slavery in the United States and African-American achievement past and present. It is celebrated by young and old alike.*

ABOVE: *A father helps his son light candles in the Kinara during Kwanzaa, a celebration that takes place each year between December 26 and January 1.*

RIGHT: *Around* 870,000 *African-American men gathered on the Mall in Washington, D.C. for the Million Man March in October* 1995.

CIVIL RIGHTS

Affirmative action emerged under the Nixon administration out of the so-called Philadelphia Plan, which ensured that federal contracts went to companies that met goals for increasing diversity by hiring African-American and other minorities, as well as women. It soon spread throughout industries and public institutions. Affirmative action policies have often helped to limit discrimination. They have also been attacked by conservative opponents and threatened by recent Supreme Court decisions. Debate, often heated, continues.

In the intervening years, the political landscape changed. African Americans began to be elected mayors of northern cities—starting in Newark, New Jersey, and Dayton, Ohio, and moving on to the big cities like Chicago, Los Angeles, New York, and Washington.

The old arguments between the separatists and the integrationists continue. One the one hand, Martin Luther King Jr.'s younger lieutenants, like Andrew Young and Jesse Jackson, have taken increasingly central roles in national politics. Jackson threw in his hat for the Democratic presidential nomination in 1984 and 1988. The voter

ABOVE: *Jesse Jackson (right) and Andrew Young have been major influences in American politics; Young as a congressmen and mayor of Atlanta, Georgia, and Jackson as a candidate for the presidential nomination.*

LEFT: *Colin Powell was appointed Secretary of State by President George W. Bush. This is one of the highest offices held by an African American.*

registration drive that he ran, attached to his campaign, attracted thousands of African Americans to vote, sometimes for the first time. Today the African-American voting bloc is a force to be reckoned with. Black politicians, such as Secretary of State Colin Powell, hold some of the highest positions in national government.

However, more radical figures also attract acclaim, support, and controversy. Some 870,000 African Americans turned out for the Million Man March in Washington, D.C. in 1995. There they listened to a two-and-a-half-hour speech by Louis Farrakhan, the leader of the Nation of Islam, urging racial pride and individual responsibility. Also speaking at this biggest civil rights march in American history were Jesse Jackson, Al Sharpton, Maya Angelou, Stevie Wonder, and Rosa Parks (*see page 62*). The event emphasized the strength of African-American communities around the country.

Yet serious problems remain. African Americans are still being beaten by white police. The video images of Rodney King's beating horrified the nation and reminded everyone of the realities of race relations. Many schools and suburbs are still segregated. What's more, the U.S. justice systems weighs heavily against African Americans— with well over one-third of African-American men in some cities in prison or on probation. It is also clear that unraveling the poverty issue from the race issue continues to be a complex and lengthy business.

TIMELINE

1619 The first 20 African Americans arrive in Jamestown, Virginia, having been captured along with a Spanish slave ship. They become indentured servants.

1641 Massachusetts becomes the first state to give legal recognition to slavery.

1644 Massachusetts passes the first law to prevent English women from marrying black men. The other colonies follow suit.

1770 Crispus Attucks is the first of five people killed in the Boston Massacre, sparking off what later became the American Revolution.

1773 The first black church is founded in Silver Bluff, South Carolina, with other black Baptist churches set up shortly thereafter in Georgia and Virginia.

1775 George Washington excludes African Americans from the Continental Army. He changes his mind after the British promised freedom to slaves who joined the British Army.

1777 Vermont becomes the first colony to abolish slavery, followed six years later by Massachusetts and New Hampshire.

1781 Los Angeles is founded in California by 44 settlers, at least 26 of them descendants of African Americans.

1793 The first fugitive slave law is passed by Congress, making it an offense to harbor escaped slaves.

1807 Congress bans the slave trade. Henceforth, slaves cannot be imported into the United States.

1810 The American Insurance Company of Philadelphia, the first African-American insurance company, is set up.

1817 Frederick Douglass is born in Talbot County, Maryland.

1827 *Freedom's Journal*, the first African-American newspaper, is published in New York City.

1831 Nat Turner's slave rebellion kills about 60 whites, and ends with his capture and execution.

LEFT: *A poster rallying African Americans to move to Nicodemus, Kansas, an all-black community founded in 1877.*

1839 The most famous slave mutiny takes place when rebels, led by Joseph Cinquez, kill the captain and take control of the slave ship *Amistad*.

1843 Presbyterian pastor Henry Highland Garnet urges the national black convention in Buffalo to lead a slave revolt.

1845 The first black lawyer, Macon B. Allen, is admitted to the bar at Worcester, Massachusetts. In the same year, the first black American diplomat, William A. Leidesdorf, is appointed subconsul to San Francisco, then in Mexican territory.

1852 Harriet Beecher Stowe's novel *Uncle Tom's Cabin* is published.

1857 The Dred Scott decision by the Supreme Court (*Scott v. Sandford*) denies African Americans the rights of citizens.

1860 The Civil War begins, and 185,000 African Americans serve in the Union Army. Nearly 38,000 are killed, and 16 win the Congressional Medal of Honor. At least a quarter of the Union Navy is African American.

1863 Abraham Lincoln signs the Emancipation Proclamation that frees slaves in the rebel states.

RIGHT: *Abraham Lincoln, who banned slavery throughout the 50 states.*

1865 The Thirteenth Amendment outlaws slavery in the United States. The House votes to ratify it 121 to 24.

1866 The much-expected plan to distribute land to freed slaves in 40-acre lots, put forward by Thaddeus Stevens, is finally defeated.

ABOVE: *The Ku Klux Klan and the White Leagues menaced African Americans in the years following the Civil War.*

1867 The first national meeting of the Ku Klux Klan occurs. Black demonstrators in Charleston force the railroad company to give everyone the right to ride in the streetcars, and similar protests occur in other cities.

1868 Representing Louisiana, John W. Menard is the first African American to be elected to Congress.

1870 Hiram R. Revels, the first African-American senator, is elected to take Jefferson Davis's seat in the Senate for Mississippi.

1874 Armed Democrats seize control of the Texas government and end the period of Radical Reconstruction there. Similar uprisings spread across the South.

1875 James A. Healy, the first black Roman Catholic bishop, is consecrated in Portland, Maine.

1881 Booker T. Washington founds the Tuskegee Institute.

1896 In *Plessy v. Ferguson*, the Supreme Court accepts the idea of "separate but equal."

1898 Louisiana's new constitution includes a so-called grandfather clause designed to exclude black voters.

1903 W. E. B. DuBois publishes *The Souls of Black Folk.*

1908 Jack Johnson defeats Tommy Burns in Australia to become heavyweight boxing champion of the world.

1909 The NAACP is founded on the centenary of Lincoln's birth.

1912 "Memphis Blues," the first published blues music, goes on sale in Memphis.

1917 The so-called Jazz Migration begins from New Orleans to Chicago.

1920 Marcus Garvey addresses 25,000 African Americans in Madison Square Garden after the launch of his Universal Improvement Association. He is imprisoned for fraud three years later.

1925 Louis Armstrong records the first Hot Five.

RIGHT: *Riots rocked Detroit during the 1960s.*

1927 Duke Ellington opens at the Cotton Club in Harlem.

1936 Jesse Owens wins four gold medals at the Berlin Olympics as Hitler watches.

1940 Benjamin Oliver Davis, Sr. becomes the first African-American general. Asa Philip Randolph threatens a march on Washington, forcing Roosevelt to ban race discrimination in the war industries.

1947 Jackie Robinson joins the Brooklyn Dodgers as the first African American in major league baseball.

BELOW: *The Count Basie Orchestra on tour.*

1954 The Supreme Court case *Brown v. Board of Education* paves the way for school integration.

1955 Rosa Parks refuses to give up her seat to a white man in Montgomery, Alabama, leading to the start of the civil rights movement.

1961 A bus with the first Freedom Riders aboard is bombed in Alabama. Martin Luther King Jr. is arrested in Atlanta. Berry Gordy launches Motown Records.

1964 Lyndon B. Johnson signs the Civil Rights Act.

1965 Malcolm X is assassinated in New York City. The Watts riot launches a wave of urban rioting.

1968 Martin Luther King Jr. is assassinated in Memphis, sparking riots in more than 100 cities.

1977 The television production of Alex Haley's novel *Roots* attracts nearly 130 million viewers.

1984 Jesse Jackson launches his first bid for the presidency.

1990 South African President Nelson Mandela addresses both houses of Congress during a barnstorming tour of the United States.

RESOURCES

BOOKS

Lerone Bennett Jr, *Before the Mayflower: A History of Black America*, 6th edition, Johnson Publishing, 1987.

Francis L. Broderick, *W. E. B. DuBois: Negro Leader in a Time of Crisis*, Stanford, 1959.

Frederick Douglass, *The Life and Times of Frederick Douglass*, Hartford, 1881.

W. E. B. DuBois, *The Souls of Black Folk*, Chicago, 1905.

Ralph Ellison, *The Invisible Man*, New York, 1952.

Adam Fairclough, *Better Day Coming: Blacks and Equality 1890–2000*, Viking Penguin, 2001.

John Hope Franklin and Alfred Moss, *From Slavery to Freedom*, McGraw-Hill, 1998.

Marcus Garvey, Amy J. Garvey (editor), and Ann Jacques Garvey (contributor), *The Philosophy and Opinions of Marcus Garvey*, Majority Press, 1986.

Henry Louis Gates Jr. and Cornel West, *The African-American Century: How Black Americans Have Shaped Our Country*, Free Press, 2000.

Kenneth S. Greenberg (editor), *Nat Turner: A Slave Rebellion in History and Memory*, Oxford University Press, 2003.

Harriet A. Jacobs, *Incidents in the Life of a Slave Girl*, Signet Classic, 2000.

Martin Luther King, Jr., *The Autobiography of Martin Luther King*, edited by Clayborne Carson, Jr., Warner, 1998.

Martin Luther King, Jr., *Where do we go from here: Chaos or Community?*, Boston, 1968.

Rosetta E. Ross, *Witnessing and Testifying: Black Women, Religion, and Civil Rights*, Fortress Press, 2003.

Harriet Beecher Stowe, *Uncle Tom's Cabin*, Oxford University Press, 2002.

Booker T. Washington, *Up from Slavery*, New York, 1901.

Malcolm X, *The Autobiography of Malcolm X*, edited by Alex Haley, New York, 1964.

MUSEUMS AND PLACES OF INTEREST

The Frederick Douglass Museum and Cultural Center
25 East Main Street, Suite 500
Rochester, New York 14614-1874
Tel: 716-546-3690
www.ggw.org/freenet/f/fdm/index.html

The Harriet Tubman Home
180 South Street
Auburn, NY 13201
Tel: 315-252-2081

Museum of Afro American History Boston
Joy Street and Smith Court
Beacon Hill
Boston, MA 02108
Tel: 617-725-0022
www.afroammuseum.org

National Underground Railroad Museum
115 East Third Street
Maysville, Kentucky 41056
Tel: 606-564-6986
www.coax.net/people/lwf/urmuseum.htm

The Troy State University Montgomery Rosa Parks
Library and Museum
251 Montgomery Street
Montgomery, AL 36104
Tel: 334-241-8661
www.tsum.edu/museum

WEB SITES

**African Americans: Culture, History, Legacy, and
Heritage of A Proud People**
www.africanamericans.com

African-American Inventors
www.inventorsmuseum.com/africanam.htm

African American Web Connection
www.aawc.com/Zaawc0.html

Africans in America
www.pbs.org/wgbh/aia

Amistad Links
www.amistad.org

Association of African-American Museums
www.blackmuseums.org

Black Facts Online
www.blackfacts.com

Black History Quest
blackquest.com/link.htm

A Deeper Shade of History: Black History Database
www.seditionists.org/black/bhist.html

The History of Jim Crow
www.jimcrowhistory.org/home.htm

The Internet African American History Challenge
www.brightmoments.com/blackhistory/

Library of Congress
www.loc.gov/exhibits/african/intro.html

North American Slave Narratives
docsouth.unc.edu/neh/nehmain.html

Pacific Bell
www.kn.pacbell.com/wired/BHM/AfroAm.html

Prominent African Americans
www.aawc.com/paa.html

Remembering Slavery: Recordings of Former Slaves
www.uncg.edu/~jpbrewer/remember

Today in Black History/Pennsylvania University
www.sas.upenn.edu/African_Studies/
K-12/Today_B_History.html

INDEX